BUSINESS MAGNATE

Why most Entrepreneurs Fail to Build a Successful Business?

COMPLETE
Business Guide

DR. RACE +VE KUMARAN
Ph.D., D.Litt. (H.C.),
Doctorate in Business Admin

INDIA · SINGAPORE · MALAYSIA

Notion Press

Old No. 38, New No. 6
McNichols Road, Chetpet
Chennai - 600 031

First Published by Notion Press 2019
Copyright © Race +ve Kumaran 2019
All Rights Reserved.

ISBN 978-1-64546-853-0

This book has been published with all efforts taken to make the material error-free after the consent of the author. However, the author and the publisher do not assume and hereby disclaim any liability to any party for any loss, damage, or disruption caused by errors or omissions, whether such errors or omissions result from negligence, accident, or any other cause.

No part of this book may be used, reproduced in any manner whatsoever without written permission from the author, except in the case of brief quotations embodied in critical articles and reviews.

Testimonial
• • •

"BUSINESS MAGNATE" is a road map to entrepreneurial success, which provides smart, practical and forward looking ideas for addressing the challenges faced by entrepreneurs in today's business environment. It is a must-read book for all those who are looking for inspiration and success in their life and business.

Brian Tracy
Author, "The Way To Wealth"

CONTENTS

Business Magnate		7
Chapter 1	Entrepreneurship	9
Chapter 2	Ready for a Business Start-Up?	24
Chapter 3	Production and Quality Assurance	46
Chapter 4	Marketing & Sales	63
Chapter 5	Goal Setting	79
Chapter 6	Planning	85
Chapter 7	Product • People • Process	91
Chapter 8	Leadership	98
Chapter 9	Sales	108
Chapter 10	Strategies Systems & Process	118
Chapter 11	Efforts & Results	133
Chapter 12	Educate, Develop & Delegate the Team	142
Chapter 13	Effective Communication Skills	149
Chapter 14	Decision Making & Delegation	157
Chapter 15	APEP – Attitude Plan Execution Performance	162
Chapter 16	Learning • Listening • Reading	167

BUSINESS MAGNATE

Welcome to the budding world of entrepreneurship, seeds that are ready to blossom as we share insights and innovations in products and services to the world at large.

BUSINESS MAGNATE leads an exploration into destinies and the purpose of life. This is a page by page guideline, a step into the future, which will enlighten entrepreneurs on steps that need to be taken to reach their ultimate goals in the frames of their lives.

Get ready to sow, reap and share!

Chapter – 1

"The true entrepreneur is a doer, not a dreamer"

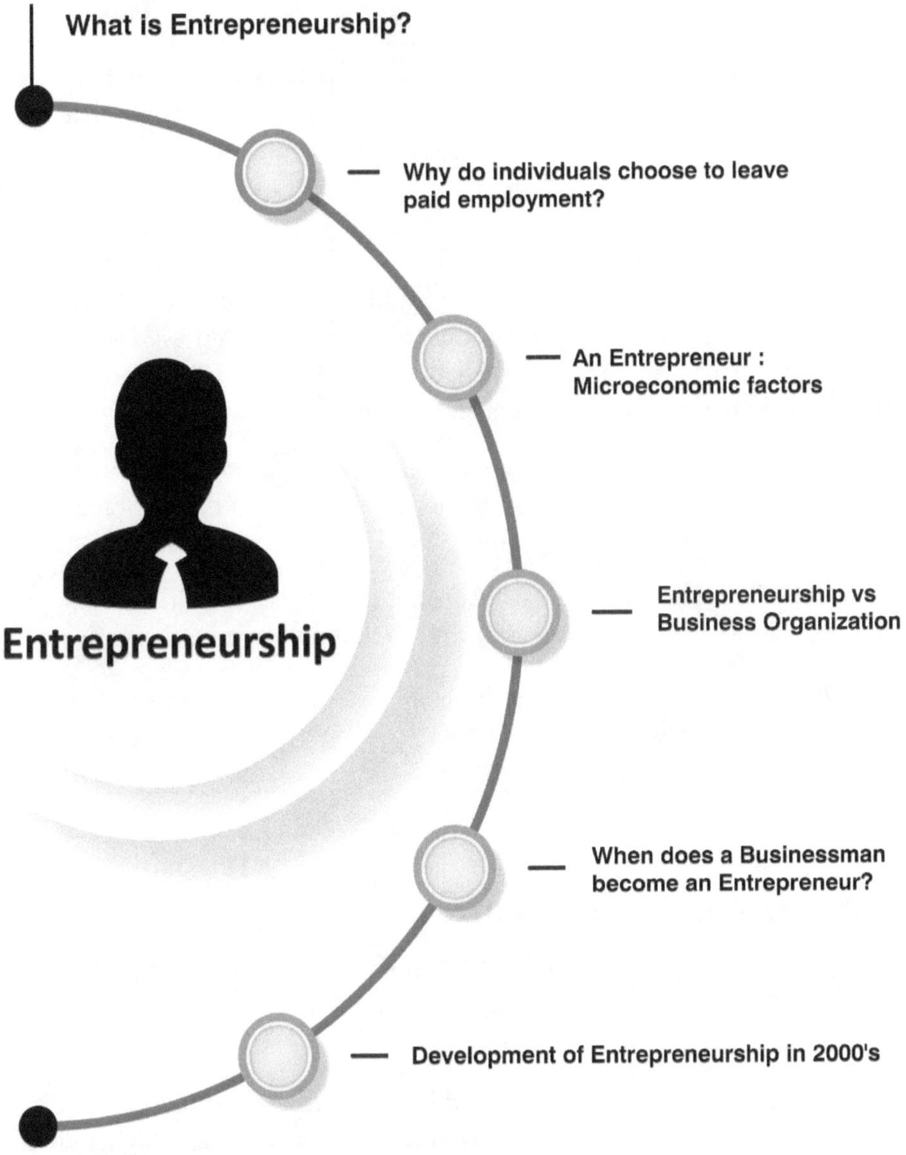

Entrepreneurship

- What is Entrepreneurship?
- Why do individuals choose to leave paid employment?
- An Entrepreneur : Microeconomic factors
- Entrepreneurship vs Business Organization
- When does a Businessman become an Entrepreneur?
- Development of Entrepreneurship in 2000's

> **Sridhar Vembu – Zoho Corporation:**
>
> Meet the CEO of Zoho Corp, Sridhar Vembu, formerly known as AdventNet Inc. This company owns Zoho online applications.
>
> AdventNet was co-founded by Sridhar Vembu in 1996 and he has been the CEO since 2000.
>
> AdventNet transformed from a fairly modest beginning to an innovative online application platform as Zoho Corporation.
>
> A multinational company dealing with the development of business software, Zoho Corporation focuses primarily on business tools that are web based and solutions related to Information Technology.
>
> The company was started by Tony Thomas and Sridhar Vembu in 1996 in California and now has offices in 7 other countries.
>
> Growing up in a middle class family in Chennai, neither of Sridhar Vembu's parents had college level education. He attended a government school until 10th standard and then did his 11th and 12th standards in another government school in English medium.
>
> He obtained an electrical engineering degree from the Indian Institute of Technology in Madras and went on to complete a Ph.D in Electrical Engineering at Princeton University.
>
> Sridhar initially worked for Qualcomm Inc as a wireless system engineer. He worked with leaders in the wireless communication industry.
>
> Zoho Corporation founded by Sridhar Vembu competes globally with Salesforce, Microsoft and Google. Zoho Corporation is valued over $1 billion.

WHAT IS ENTREPRENEURSHIP?

"The entrepreneurial seed is the initial urge to turn a passion into profit. The journey is initiated when a concept is set forth and transforms dreams into a reality!"

A 19th-century French economist defined entrepreneurship as: "Shifting economic resources from lower to higher areas of productivity and higher yield."

"Entrepreneur" is a word borrowed from the French language. It appeared in a French dictionary, published in 1723 by Jacques des Bruslons. The equivalent word in British English is "Adventurer."

Entrepreneurship studies date back into the 17th and 18th Centuries by Irish-French economist Richard Cantillon. Cantillon viewed entrepreneurs as risk takers who deliberately allocated resources in order to exploit opportunities with the aim to maximise financial returns. He emphasised the entrepreneur's willingness to assume risk uncertainties and drew attention to entrepreneurial functions and clearly distinguished the difference between entrepreneurs and funders. During the German medieval guild, a craftsperson required permission for entrepreneurship operation. Only craftspeople who were Meister certified were allowed training as apprentices. Thiswas introduced after the Gewerbefreiheit free trade in 1871. Earlier, there was no need to prove competence in order to start a business. Then in later years, from1935 to 1953, there was a need for proof of competence. Craftspeople had to get certified before getting permission to set-up any business as such.

ENTREPRENEURSHIP IN THE 20TH CENTURY

The 20th century gave rise to studies by Austrian economist Joseph Schumpeter, Ludwig von Mises and Carl Menger as well as Friedrich von Hayek.

The word **entrepreneur** may have had its initial French roots in the 1850's, but around the1920's, it evolved. Schumpeter defined an entrepreneur as one who is willing and able to convert new inventions or ideas into successful innovations.

Schumpeter referred to it as **'creative destruction'** which replaces inferior offerings across industries and markets, creates new business models and new products leading to economic growth on a long-term basis.

The statement that 'entrepreneurship leads to growth in an economy' is often debated in academic forums.

Entrepreneurship results in new innovative combinations with existing inputs and new industries. An example by Schumpeter refers to a steam engine and wagons replacing horse-drawn carriages.

Then innovation like cars not only replaced carriages, but also led to the auto industry of modern times with improvements and reduction in associated costs due to technology.

However microeconomic theories set in tradition considered theoretical frameworks within entrepreneurial settings with the entrepreneur seen as an unspecified actor.

Schumpeter did not see entrepreneurs as bearing any risk; he saw them as capitalist as such. He believed that equilibrium was not perfect and continuously changing environments provided a new stream of incoming information linking to optimum use of resources.

Some individuals get new information ahead of others and combine resources to gain entrepreneurial profit.

Schumpeter rated entrepreneurial shift to higher levels of production possibilities with the use of innovation.

Economists attempted the study of entrepreneurship and viewed entrepreneurs as capitalists who were multi-tasking in a competitive market as creators of economic activity.

LET US TALK ABOUT THE LANDSCAPE OF ENTREPRENEURSHIP

This is where fresh ideas, solutions, pathways, structures and formats are realised through a lesson plan or composition, a business venture or a proposal for a project.

The landscape becomes a robust space that is filled with passionate spirits creating wonders in the universe.

Business success is connected to creativity in its existence. This is an aspect very often overlooked. Strategy and a form of organisation is the foreground for business success, no denying that it in this competitive modern world, innovation is the key. And innovation has its roots in creativity. New ideas are dependent on creativity to be successfully implemented. This connection gets lost when there is an overflow of abundant creativity but no implementation.

WHO IS AN ENTREPRENEUR?

Entrepreneurs are managers who oversee the launch of a product or concept and monitor its growth. An individual or a team identifies a possible business opportunity and then sets forth to acquire all the resources required to exploit the idea.

Entrepreneurs create something different or something new. They change values.

Whether a company is small or big, partaking in entrepreneurship is always an open door.

What it takesto successfully delve into the world of entrepreneurship?

Becoming an entrepreneur has 4 needed criteria:

1. Situation or opportunities must be available to recombine available resources and generate a profit.
2. Entrepreneurship requires preferential access to creative individuals or the ability to recognise opportunities.
3. Thirdly, RISKS are inherently present.
4. People and resources need to be organised.

WHY DO INDIVIDUALS CHOOSE TO LEAVE PAID EMPLOYMENT?

These are some relevant pointers:

Advantages of Quitting Paid Employment:

- You have more control over the kind of work you choose to do.
- Your work schedule is flexible and at a location of your choice.
- Many feel that their skills are wasted when employed at a corporation and potential remains unfulfilled.

- Escaping from an uninteresting career or job.
- Desire to pursue a hobby to interest.
- Be your own boss.

Disadvantages of Quitting Paid Employment:
- You are solely responsible for all that goes wrong.
- Financial pressure, unstable income.
- Work harder than conventional jobs.
- Multi-tasking.
- No leave on sick days.
- Emotional rollercoaster.

Success Methods Predictors:
- Establish strategies.
- Maintain human resource by recruiting talent and retaining valuable employees.
- Ensure availability of materials required.
- Ensure the firm has competitive advantages that are unique.
- Ensure governance, organisational design and organisational coordination.
- Business to consider N2C or business-to-business models.
- Target customers or markets that are untapped or missed by others.
- Utilisestate-of-the-technology.
- Focus on growing industry.
- Ensure there is an adequate capital inflow.

Team Composition:
- Gender diverse.
- Racial diverse.

- Multiple talents.
- Graduate degrees.
- Experience.
- Full-time employment.
- Entrepreneurial Experience.
- Motivated by goals and not just profit.
- Business networks.

Company Profile:

- Business Plan.
- Connected service or product line.
- Project completion based on service or quality and not price.
- Well-targeted marketing plans evolved on a regular basis.
- Financial control.
- Sufficient growth capita.
- Start-up costs and cash flow issues need to be strategised.

AN ENTREPRENEUR: A MICROECONOMIC FACTOR

Entrepreneurship studies date back to works of Adam Smith and Richard Cantillon. This was as early as the 17th century and beginning of the 18th century. Entrepreneurship was theoretically ignored until the 19th and 20th centuries emerged.

This was when profound business resurgence and economics took effect. The 20th century understanding of entrepreneurship is based largely on the work on Joseph Schumpeter, a 1930's economist. Other economists making waves include Carl Menger Friedrich von Hayek and Ludwig von Mises.

Schumpeter defined an entrepreneur as a person willing to convert an idea or an invention into innovation that succeeds.

Creative disruption replaces inferior innovations across industries and markets, creating brand new products and business models. Industry dynamism and economic growth are rooted from creative disruption.

Entrepreneurship leading to economic growth is a hotly debated topic in the economics academia. Many innovations result in improvements, but sometimes it is like replacing paper straws with plastic.

Characteristics of Successful Entrepreneurs:

- Entrepreneurs that are successful follow key pathways:
- Develop a business plan.
- Hire human resources.
- Acquire material and financial resources.
- Provide leadership.
- Take full responsibility for failure or success of the venture.
- Plan for Risk Aversion.
- Any healthy economy needs innovative entrepreneurs.

The Entrepreneurship Ecosystem:

- Entrepreneurship in charitable organisations and government:
- Entrepreneurship operates within government services and programs that promote economic development through start-ups and entrepreneur support.
- Non-governmental associations like small business organisations and associations offering advice and mentoring entrepreneurs.
- Advocacy organisations and small businesses lobby governments for entrepreneurship support.

Facilities and Resources:

- Training programs and education for entrepreneurs by universities schools and colleges.
- Financing through venture capital, bank loans and grants.

THE DIFFERENCE BETWEEN ENTREPRENEURSHIP AND BUSINESS ORGANISATION

Defining entrepreneurship is about identifying opportunities, evaluating them and then deciding to exploit them.

New services and products are developed as well as new industries and companies formed to create wealth.

The process of entrepreneurship is uncertain, as opportunities are not discovered until actualisation

For an opportunity to be actualised as *business, financial and social capital is required.* Business opportunities are perceived by entrepreneurs. They have a risk-taking tendency.

Businessmen walk on defined logistical paths; entrepreneurs make their own path and create a guideline for businessmen. It is a misconception that entrepreneurs and businessmen fall within exact definitions. They may be used interchangeably but differ in outlook.

A businessman runs a business undertaking an idea that is not original. An entrepreneur initiates a service or product and becomes a leader in the created market.

In essence, an entrepreneur evolves into a businessman but with a difference. There is a fine line between the terms. An entrepreneur is a leader in the market, while a businessman is basically a market player.

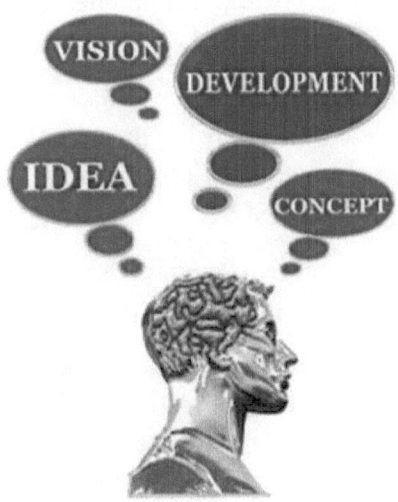

BUSINESSMAN vs ENTREPRENEUR

- A businessman sets up business in an existing context offering services and products.
- An entrepreneur initiates a commercial venture with a new concept or undertaking.
- A businessman is a market player.
- An entrepreneur is a market leader.
- A businessman is calculative.
- An entrepreneur is intuitive.
- A businessman takes low risk.
- An entrepreneur takes high risk.
- A businessman applies conventional methods.
- An entrepreneur is unconventional.
- A businessman is profit driven.
- An entrepreneur is people driven.

When Does a Businessman Become an Entrepreneur?:

There is a relationship between small businesses and entrepreneurship, used interchangeably small businesses and entrepreneurship are often terms that are conflated.

Entrepreneurship ventures may start off as small businesses but not every small business is entrepreneurial in nature. Small businesses are made up of operations through sole proprietorship that may have a few employees.

These businesses offer products, services or processes that are existing. They are not aiming at growth.

Entrepreneurial ventures offer new product, services or processes and an entrepreneur aims to scale up the company by adding employees venturing to seek international sales, etc. This process needs venture capital or angel investments. Successful entrepreneurs lead a business in a positive direction with proper planning, adapting to changing landscapes in the business world and by understanding their strengths or weaknesses.

DEVELOPMENT OF ENTREPRENEURSHIP IN THE 2000's

Entrepreneurship extended in origins from non-profit enterprises and included social entrepreneurship. Business goals link to environmental, social and humanitarian goals. And there is even the political entrepreneur term Entrepreneurship within existing large organisations are termed "intrapreneurship" and include corporate ventures that larger entities create through subsidiary organisations.

Entrepreneurs are:

- Leaders
- Risk takers
- Exercise initiative
- Take advantage of opportunities
- Effective planning, effective organising and then deploying resources
- Self employed

There are Basically 3 Types of Entrepreneurial Mindsets:

- Social entrepreneurship
- Political Entrepreneurship
- Knowledge Entrepreneurship

Depending on creativity and organisation types, entrepreneurs range in scale. They can be single, have part time or large scale projects involving teams and creating employment.

High cost ventures need venture capital or seed money otherwise known as angel investment to expand and raise capital for businesses.

There are many organisations and government agencies set-up to support entrepreneurs.

These are business incubators, which may be for-profit or not or operated by educational institutions that can be like NGOs or science parks. These may include charities, advocacy groups or foundations.

Ethnic Entrepreneurship:

Self employed individuals within minority population groups in Europe or the US are referred to as ethnic entrepreneurs.

Ethnic entrepreneurship has been included in academia research syllables in the US, which explore strategies and experiences of ethic entrepreneurs as they integrate into mainstream economics in Western societies.

Classic examples include Jewish traders and merchants in US cities during the 19th and 20th Centuries as well as Japanese and Chinese businesses set-up in the Western world.

Studies of 2010 ethnic entrepreneurship cases in the US covered various ethnic groups including Cuban business leaders in Miami, Chinese business and Indian owners of motels. (A case study on ethnic entrepreneurship in 2010 included Cuban business leaders in Miami, Chinese business and Indian owners of motels).

Ethnic entrepreneurship offers opportunities or self-employment and economic advancement, but there is an imbalance in terms of uneven racial and ethnic distribution.

There have been multiple success stories on entrepreneurs from Asia, but statistics reveal whites are more likely to have self-employed status in lucrative and prestigious industries.

Cultural Entrepreneurship:

Cultural entrepreneurship is based on personalities or individuals who build their own creativity brand as cultural authority. This is used to leverage, sustain and create cultural enterprises.

Entrepreneurs that build a substantial amount of cult within cultural spheres, force synergies in political, cultural, industrial and philanthropic interest as well as collective enterprises to engage in cultural productions and services which may be for-profit in some cases.

Feminist Entrepreneurship:

An entrepreneur who applies feminist approaches and values through entrepreneurship with an ultimate goal of improving life quality and well-being of women and girls.

Social Entrepreneurship:

When start-up companies and entrepreneurs fund, develop and implement social environment and cultural solution, they are known as social entrepreneurs.

This concept can be applied to various organisations that have differing aims, beliefs and sizes. A for-profit entrepreneur's performance is measured in metrics of business terminology such as revenues, profit and stock price increase.

Social entrepreneurs are not-for-profit or have a system that provides positive rewards for society within different metrics.

Social entrepreneurship attempts to broaden cultural, social and environmental goals that are associated with voluntary sectors within areas of poverty alleviation, community development and health care.

Social enterprises that are profit making are established to support cultural and social goals and not for self-gain. For example, an organisation supporting homeless people may have an establishment set-up like a restaurant to raise money for providing employment and housing.

Nascent Entrepreneur:

This term refers to an individual in the process of establishing a business venture through pursuing an opportunity to introduce new products or services, serve new developments as well as markets and develop efficient methods of production to make a profit.

The opportunity pursued by a nascent entrepreneur is perceived. Ignited by such personal beliefs and the action undertaken by a nascent entrepreneur will define the establishment of the venture.

The novice entrepreneur, the serial entrepreneur and the portfolio entrepreneur are examples of behaviour-based categories.

Nascent entrepreneurs embark on a series of activities and not a solitary act of a single opportunity.

Interrelationships exist between the activity and knowledge is acquired in order to form an opportunity base. With this research, scholars will be able to begin constructing a theory of the micro-foundations of entrepreneurial action leading to emergence of a new venture.

These actions proceed to make the business venture concrete. There is a search for equipment and facilities, legal entities are formed and energy as well as time is dedicated to the business.

Project-Based Entrepreneurs:

Individuals engaged in repeating the formation of temporary organisations that have a limited lifespan and devoted to singular goals as well as objectives are known as project-based entrepreneurs.

Industries within this sector include sound recording, filmmaking, software development, new media, television production and construction.

These temporary ventures have to be modified and recreated on an ongoing basis to suit emerging new project needs. Business models are modified as such to suit emerging new projects.

There is exposure to repeat problems on tasks in the entrepreneurial process and there are critical challenges that invariably characterise new venture creations.

These include: Locating the opportunity for launching the project venture and assembling an appropriate team to exploit the opportunity.

Resolving this challenge requires access to extensive information to seize new opportunities for investment. Resolving the second challenge requires the assembling of a collaborative team that can fit within a particular challenge of the venture to function with immediate effect and reduce performance risk that may adversely affect the project.

One other project entrepreneurship type is when an entrepreneur utilises students to get ideas analysed.

Millennial Entrepreneur:

Millennial entrepreneur refers to a business owner in affiliate mass media and digital technology.

These business owners are equipped with new technology knowledge. The business models have a strong grasp of technology applications.

Many breakthrough businesses have emerged from the millennial era such as Facebook.

Despite overambitious assumptions and doubt regarding expectation of success of millennial entrepreneurs, recent studies have proven such ventures as successful. Economic barriers, education debt and challenges are main aspects distinguishing between millennial and the rest in the current generation.

Behavioural Entrepreneur:

The entrepreneur is the individual who initiates a new idea by creating instruments of innovation for new business processes.

Note: Irrespective of what type an entrepreneur is classified as, team building and management skills are perceived as essential for leadership in the world of entrepreneurs.

INTROSPECTION QUESTIONNAIRE

1. What criteria are required to become an entrepreneur?

   _____
   _____

2. Is it advisable for salary classed people to quit their jobs and start-up a business to become an entrepreneur?

   _____
   _____

3. What are the similarities and differences between a businessman and an entrepreneur?

   _____
   _____

Chapter – 2

*"Don't wait for the perfect moment...
take the moment and make it perfect"*

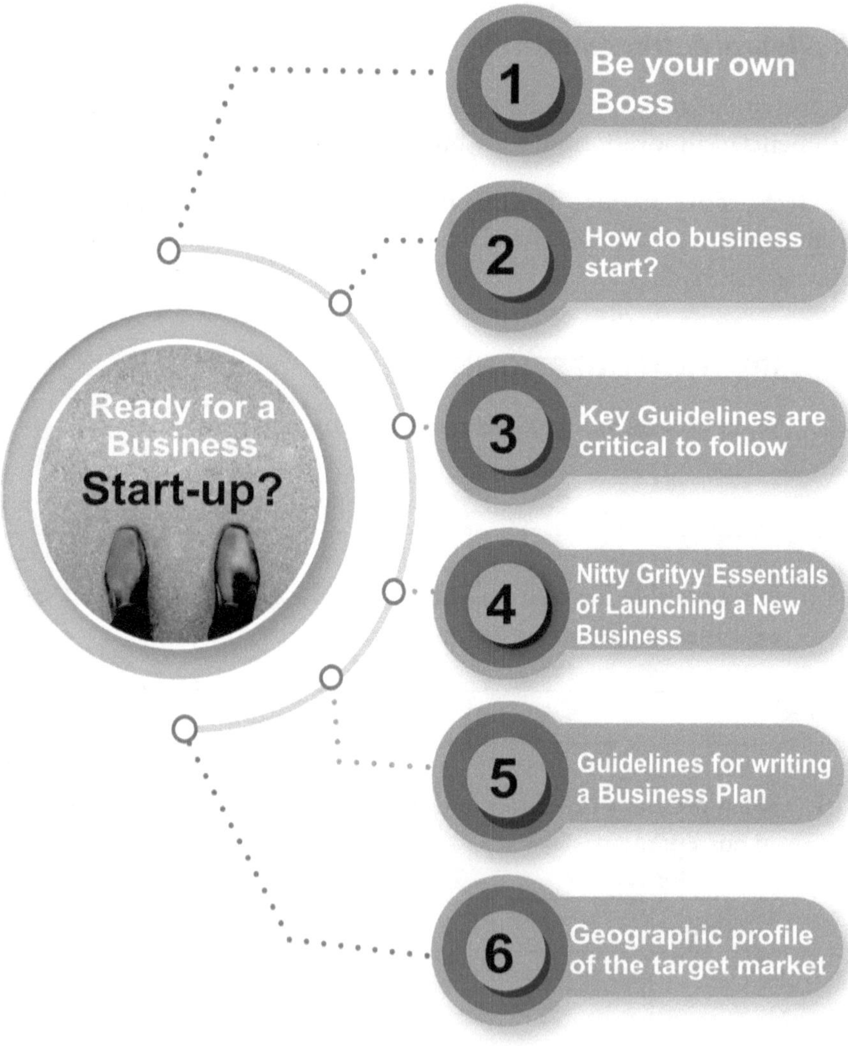

Ready for a Business Start-up?

1. Be your own Boss
2. How do business start?
3. Key Guidelines are critical to follow
4. Nitty Grityy Essentials of Launching a New Business
5. Guidelines for writing a Business Plan
6. Geographic profile of the target market

Dr. Arokiaswamy Velumani – Thryocare:

Dr. Arokiaswamy Velumani lived above a lab in Mumbai and most often slept in his lab. Today this son of a poor farmer is worth millions in assets through his venture Thyrocare Technologies Limited.

Early life of Dr. Arokiaswamy Velumani.

He was born in an obscure village in Tamil Nadu and had little hope for bright future ahead.

His life of penury meant that his schooling and college education were supported by government scholarships.

Today he owns the largest thyroid testing centre in the world, boasting of over 1,122 outlets all over India as well as the Middle East. His career started in a small pharmaceutical company called Gemini Capsules. He earned a low monthly salary. When the company closed down Velumani lost his job.

Never one to give up easily, he landed a job in Bhabha Atomic Research Centre in Mumbai where he worked for 14 years.

He eventually embarked on his own venture. His thyroid biochemistry expertise led him to create a testing lab for detecting thyroid disorders.

He had some capital from his provident fund of Rs. 100,000. Velumani was 37 years of age when he launched his venture in Byculla, South Mumbai.

Thyrocare is now worth Rs. 3,377 crore with Velumani owning 64 per cent share thus making him worth Rs. 2,158 crore!

Velumani is not sitting on his laurels as Thyrocare is now working on developing another subsidiary for cancer screening via molecular imaging process.

"Are you happy doing what you do to earn a living? Think about it… Yes?

Kind of?

Maybe?

There are ups and downs in the journey of your life and work. But think for instance are you everyday dragging yourself out of your bed at 8 a.m. or 9 a.m. to sprint to your work station and sprinting back home as soon as the clock strikes 5 p.m. Are you satisfied with your routine or looking out for a change.

We spend hours each day in an office work station or other setups to earn our monthly wages to pay bills and fulfil other needs. There needs to be some passion and inspiration in the day-to-day routine journey of life. If you have the talent, an idea, or a passion, it is time to do some research and start a business!

Take the plunge! Start your own!

BE YOUR OWN BOSS

Starting a business gives a brand new level of freedom. You will have to incorporate ethics and morals in the process of decision making. You can pick your time to work, you can decide what you want to work on, where you choose to work and what you wear. How does that sound?

When you have a great idea, a unique service to offer or a new set of unique recipes, a product you believe no one should miss out on, there is this driving force and compelling energy to launch a new business.

Your time, your money and your future can level off to launch into the known or the unknown. Keeping a rational eye and all failures in a row, there is no reason to forsake the everlasting success and turn it into a reality into the beyond.

Time to Say Goodbye to Boring 9 to 5 Jobs!:

You are the key to your emancipation in a world of free choices. Determine your pathway with self-identification and break down inner personalities that define who we are as individuals.

We are all very different as individuals. Some are early risers and can start working before the sun rises. Others are like night owls but need to stay in bed until lunchtime and can go on working through the night with no supervision from the boss or prying eyes of colleagues.

There is flexibility in being your own boss. You can juggle family time, time for pets and socialising too. There is no need to worry about finding a baby sitter or rushing home in heavy traffic!

But there are constant challenges in being your own boss. Each day is different and you are constantly learning, gaining skills and meeting people. So there will never be boring days! Your work is your life and you need to be running it!

A business deal is more than just great service and product. Just like a new born child, it has a life force that has needs and requirements to survive, co-exist and thrive in the circle of its existence.

You have take it on as mission to plan ideas and processes. Getting ready to start your own business is a personal decision with long-lasting and wide-ranging consequences. Do not enter into it unprepared or lightly. Keep a knowledgeable guide or mentor by your side. Be willing to embrace downsides as well if all does not pan out as envisioned.

Doing What You Love:

Work will always be work. Doing what you love is rewarding. Starting a business will involve blood, sweat and tears. Now when you venture into following your passion, work hours fly by and your enthusiasm becomes contagious.

Prospective customers, funders and partners can be swept away by your strong vision. Follow your vision, find the gap in the market while doing what you love as a businessman and make a living out of it.

Creative:

Be creative when planning to start your own business as a creativity gives you artistic freedom. You can decide what you want to do and when you want to do it. Share what you are good at and show people your true potential. There is no reason for you to follow another person's vision, but be sure to meet requirements of clients.

Whether you are good at photography or making tasty brownies, or maybe you just love the thrill of setting up a business, make sure you a vision for launching a creative spark that can ignite your bright and healthy future.

If you have checked out the territory of your interest, researched the idea, evaluated the market and customers, there is nothing can hold you back from launching your very own business. Life is short and it is better to do what you care about, so if you have a good idea come out with it.

Everyone wants to be remembered for something in their life. And by starting a business it could fulfil that desire. Whether it is the most successful start-up or the biggest failure, you leave behind a legacy.

And a failure is never a failure as such. It is a new lesson that will help launch your next initiative with even more success. Many creative ideas are not fulfilled when working for others. Employees don't get enough creative freedom and feel limited. Creativity needs flexibility and freedom.

You need to decide the pathway of your destiny. You can keep asking yourself if others can do it, why not I then the world will be filled with possibilities. It is up to you to follow all that can open up for you in that world of possibilities.

Fulfil Goal:

A magical entrepreneurship quality seems to be that all must be figured out before the launch of a venture? This is not true. No one can have all issues figured out before the launch of a venture. There will always be some jump into extraordinary situations. Even established organisations have suffered struggles and victories together with lessons learnt from such incidents.

These are inevitable elements in a process. Like every other aspect of life, it comes with trials and tribulations. There is no need to have special entrepreneurial genes. If you have a strong desire to do something, then you have to believe in it and make a plan to achieve it.

Follow basic steps to get started and create a route map so that people you hire also follow it to achieve your avowed goal.

Define the Business:

It is essential to define a business specifically and goals needed to be outlined to set-up a successful business.

You need to know if you are on track so list what you have in mind along with your target audience. Then outline how will you reach your target audience? How do you plan to work with your target audience?

If you are a designer, for example, a passionate creator of products that suits people, then it will be great to meet a customer personally. But if they are not within proximity to personally meet you, then you can effectively communicate through online media. Discover the persona and strategy behind the person you are working for and that will define the design you are going to prepare.

Name Your Business:

Your business is like your new baby. You need to send the baby into the world by giving it a name. It should be specific telling people what you do, but also be broad enough to give it room for expansion. It is an exciting and challenging part of starting a business. Once done you feel proud and legitimate.

Legalise It:

It is imperative to make the business official and legal. Choose a legal entity and pay the requisite fee to complete formalities. In case anything wrongs occurs, it can help shield your personal assets and finances. Get all the paperwork done and choose an appropriate agency to facilitate it.

Open a Business Banking Account:

It will take time to get legal paperwork done but once it is done, it is an imperative step forward step to start a bank account for the business. You need to do this in order to keep your personal finances apart from your business expenses, which will make a big difference. Your personal account should be separated and kept safely away from your business transactions.

Invest in Branding:

Once a business is defined and you are established, you need to focus on brand building. Brand building helps the business to stand out and adds credibility. This then draws your dream target audience and builds trust.

Brand building in the right way gives the business a face that can make you proud, empower you and sell your creative endeavours with confidence.

Setting Up Systems:

By setting up systems, you save time and brain power. Systems ensure that you do not flout rules including banking norms.

Billing:

Decide how you will be collecting payments, it can be cash, cheque, credit card, net banking or other forms of electronic modes such as PayPal.

Contracts:

If you need contracts in your business, make sure you have a template. You can save clients the hassle of printing, scanning and also get an e-signature process to save on your time as well.

Accounting and Tracking:

Keep a proper track of your expenses and income. This makes the tax process much easier and there are many digital platforms available to plan your accounting system.

Project Management:

Managing projects online can sometimes be a nightmare. Try workflow processes or apps linked to your line of business that can make the system of managing projects faster and easier.

Marketing:

Get a system in place to market your products; also decide on your advertising plans whether it is print, electronic or social media platforms. Define the media platform that will reach a large audience. Define which social media platforms can reach your targeted clients, what do you post and how often do you post. There are many platforms in this day and age, target the ones that will be best for your business. There are methods to organise and schedule posts. Once these steps are in order you can sell the magic and dazzle the world with all that you have to offer.

Remember you can do this once you are firmly set in your mind, believe in yourself and reject all those who advice otherwise.

HOW DO BUSINESSES START? OUTSOURCERS TO SMALL BUSINESSES

They start with an idea, a spark. A what if?

This momentary vision shifts the business ignition to the brain.

An idea is the first step. There is a minute first step. If every great idea is translated into a profitable business, all would be entrepreneurs.

Some ideas can be viable and some not. Others need faith and funding.

Knowing the difference is by asking you the toughest questions to expose the weaknesses within the idea. Or they may reveal all the hidden strengths.

The kind of questions within the sphere are:

"Do you have experience in this sector of the industry?"

"Or who will be interested in purchasing the product or using the service?"

Okay, you have been there and done that. Years and years of what seemed like eternity staying in a large established company as an employee. But then the time has arrived and you have decided to go at it alone. This is fantastic. Now the movement forward is taking the next step to turn the free thinking idea of being an outsources into a small business. This is step 2 of the process.

KEY GUIDELINES ARE CRITICAL TO FOLLOW

Have the Right Mindset:

Starting any business is not easy. Be sure of your inner personality. Analyse yourself. Know if you can deal with highs and lows. Without a doubt, there will be loads of work. Besides the service or product aspect, there is administration and project management as well.

Work Flow:

You have to be sure that you have a constant work flow. Without work, there is no income. You need finances for your business to progress and grow.

If this is not the case, rather consider remaining an outsourcer until you have a better and constant workload. Judge it on a monthly basis to ensure that the workload remains stable. If you have a working surplus then maybe passing work onto other outsourcers is a good start for launching a business.

Cash Flow:

Funds are an important factor for the success of any business, big or small. Maybe being an outsourcer for a while gives you some savings to launch your own business. But there are extra expenses to consider such as rent, utilities, catering and business insurance. Small businesses and start-ups are the most vulnerable when it comes to problems of cash flow. Some reasons for cash flow vulnerabilities:

The first round of sales can take a while and this gestation period comes with incurring costs with little revenue inflow.

Components suppliers can start demanding early payments from initial start-up business that have not yet developed a track record of paying their bills on time.

A business that is new has to pay upfront for product development and marketing promotion.

There will be no cash reserves from retained profits to source these finances.

Initial stages of start-up business face challenges of cash flow management.

Without proper planning and management of cash flow, businesses start to dwindle resulting in the possibility of failure.

Cash Flow Steps to Follow:

Work though finances carefully! Do you have a cash flow to cover the start-up costs? Where do you source additional funds from? Analyse what your profits and losses will be.

Consider hiring freelancers or part-timers rather than taking on full-time employees in case there is a funds crunch. Review the business plan and double check to ensure that you have covered all the bases especially with regards to funding and finances.

Be realistic. Be thorough. Small businesses fail because of a lack of cash flow.

Think of cash flow as the lifeblood of a business. Start-up business owners need to forecast cash flow direction to ensure they can keep operating. It might be detrimental to a business it there is no proper cash flow management. Make it a point to identify possible shortfalls in advance. The forecast of cash flow should be a system of an early warning.

The business must be able to afford payments to employees as well as suppliers and other vendors involved in the business.

Analyse Customer Payments:

Evaluate the debt system process if you offer services or goods on credit. This does not apply to cash on point of sale methods. Financial planning is imperative. Preparing budgets is crucial to the management process stakeholders and funders usually require forecasts on a regular basis.

Training Employees:

If you decided to quit your previous job as your ideas were compromised, then think about having to train new people and how you would feel about getting inputs from them on your concepts. If you would rather do things your own way, ensure you have clear processes that are in place.

As the company develops into further advancement there are various pathways ahead for development. It is important to provide a foundation in order to grow as a business; the owner should endeavour to bring experts to train employees. Training from experts will allow new trends in an emergency.

Optimise Strength of Employees:

During initial phases begin a general training program. Allow employees to grow into roles that they can specialise in. In a start-up business, all employees should be able to explore all setups. This will build a strong foundation, nurturing skills of the team and ensuring competence at all levels of the organisation.

Set-Up e-Learning Programmes:

The platform of e-learning is an effective method to gather knowledge and insight. Consider an e-learning programme to train employees. It is an imperative platform in the growing techno – savvy era. A typical e-learning lesson can contain multiple choice questions, puzzles, fill in the blanks, essays, and games. Each lesson can have a quiz attached. Completing sequences can earn employees some incentives.

Give Employees Tasks for Training:

Employees can learn effectively when they have a hands-on task. Training has to be an in-house experience; it is a platform for self-education and practical application. This enhances theoretical lessons and workshop programmes.

Encourage Expertise Sharing:

Hold monthly sessions where experts share areas of aspects they specialise in. This helps to share skills for effectively building a diverse team of effective leaders.

NITTY GRITTY ESSENTIALS OF LAUNCHING A NEW BUSINESS

Once you have decided to enter the business world, you will have to choose a name for your business name and your brand, chalk out a business plan and register the business. The next big task will be sorting out finances!

All good points for setting up a new business: Starting your own business is a massive achievement that you will be proud of! Because you are going to do what you love. Hiring people will have to follow from a bigger pool of talent.

The Not so good points in setting up a business: More Risk, more costs with more staff and bigger responsibility. There will also be extra work and no rolling funds in initial stages. No guarantee all will work if you are ready to launch a new business, get a business plan in order. And plan on how to get finances to make your dreams a reality.

GUIDELINES FOR WRITING A BUSINESS PLAN

Why Do You Need a Business Plan?:

Even if friends and family are financing your business, a business plan is a necessity. A business plan is not just a tool for fundraising, it is much more. It is for you to understand your overall business. It is to monitor progress, be in control, hold yourself accountable and control the fate of the business. It is also a tool for sales and recruitment, getting key employees and future investors as well.

Writing a business plan ensures regular review of value proposition, operation plan, staffing plan and supporting requirements which present opportunities but you might otherwise miss.

The operational plan will lay out crucial milestones in all aspects. The founder of any business is accountable for results on a daily basis, so a business plan becomes the baseline to monitor progress.

You witness breakthroughs. You see heroic efforts, you see over estimations as you progress and do a better job in future with a good business plan.

A plan drives the future pathway of the business. When you state that you expect one hundred clients by the end of a year, it is not just a passive prediction. As you do not just expect those clients to enter by wishful thinking, it becomes a goal for the sales and marketing team.

The plan states and executes targets in each major area. Expenditure, sales, hiring and financial matters are all clearly laid down so that they become the goals of performance.

When your business needs to be understood, the plan provides an overall overview. A plan that is well written will, in turn, attract the right talent. When a prospective investor asks for an understanding of your business, you then hand them a business plan that provides an entire overview.

The reactions you get indicate how thoroughly and how fast the reader can visualise the key business issues that you have iterated. Written records coupled with your delivery track record send a clear and loud message that you understand your business as well as you can deliver promised results. Great employees then respond to the message along with investors and banks when you need to raise money. Again viewing the business plan as a tool for fundraising is just the beginning of what a business plan is all about.

A business plan can also help you in the recruiting process as well as operating and managing your business well too. You can consider the implications of your business plan and it will definitely prove worthy of the time that you have invested.

Potential investors should not be left confused, they should feel confident about returns on their investment. Whether you need investment or not, writing a business plan is essential to stay on track. If you do need funding, potential investors will need to know what they are investing in.

A Business Plan Consists of 6 Sections:

- Executive Summary
- Vision
- Marketing and Target Market
- Operations
- People
- Finances

Executive Summary: Any prospective investor reads the summary first, before deciding to invest more time into any further reading. This summary defines if the project is a worthwhile investment.

Keep the executive summary short and provide a clear outline of your business. Give the reader a clear and simple introduction. Your elevator statement and proposition should be presented in one sentence. Address problems present in the market and how you aim to solve them as well as how you propose to fulfil customers' needs.

Elaborate on needs as well as problems and why you decided to start that particular business.

Include business milestones and avowed goals for the year. This is an opportunity for giving an overview of predicted revenue as well as profit.

This part of the plan is a synopsis, short, and memorable. This should be the final step of a business plan and write this part last once you have all the other information in place.

Vision: Introducing business detail. Where is it currently located and your visualisation of its progress?

Explain why the business is needed. What is its purpose? What problems does the business seek to solve?

What is unique about the business?

Why will potential customers spend money on the product?

List 5 key features to make your concept different. This is crucial.

- Provide in-depth detail on copyright, intellectual property, patents and related issues.
- You should have detailed information to defend your idea without any iota of doubt.
- Analyse current trends and see if you are ready for the market.
- Define the time frame for your business and your future plans for trading.
- Explain the growth potential for your product and explain that future plans are intact.

Investors Evaluate Business History: Is it taken over business and ready for re-launch or is it starting from scratch?

Outline goals to be implemented to reach the overall vision and annual targets. Do not stretch yourself beyond limits and examine all information carefully when you document it.

Is the business set-up as a limited company, a sole proprietor or partnership? These questions need to be addressed as well as what changes will occur in the future.

Marketing: Describe the marketing strategy clearly. Identify channels to reach your potential customers and analyse market conditions. Study trends and positions to analyse how your product or service fits into that particular market.

Operations: Know your customers through your team: Teams make up a crucial component of any business. Include details of role players in your team, their credibility and profiles. Describe how they are suited to roles. Describe the skill sets and past achievement and how it relates to current duties.

People: Make sure that you invest in the right people as you and your team are one of the most important aspects of your business. If there are certain required skills that your current team does not possess, outsource them. This can include lawyers, freelance experts and accountants. When you outsource make sure that you provide relevant information of your business to get best results from outsourcers.

Finances: Not everybody can get into the world of numbers, but understanding them is essential. Running costs, forecasts of profit and loss, sales and cash flow are keys to identify. For the purpose of your plan, your finances should comprise of 2 sections: The daily running costs of the company and forecasts for sales, profit and loss as well as cash flow.

Financial plans need to be worked out for a minimum of 3 years and should include when the business will break even as well as when the business is most likely to make profit.

It is no easy task to detail everything, but make sure to account for as much as possible from rent, electricity, gas, water bills, salaries, internet, vendor payments, miscellaneous expenses, catering or pantry expenses to incentives for staff.

Indicate revenue streams as well as forecasts of projected profits and losses.

Prepare contingency plans for costly raw materials. Do not overstretch and be realistic with numbers.

Challenge yourself and remain confident of delivery. Indicate how you have arrived at predicted figures. Include total needed funding and how you aim to get it. Outline what investors will gain in return from your 'killer' proposal!

It is vital that plans are well written. People will not be impressed with an ill-written, unchecked document filled with errors.

You do not need to devise a boring formal plan. Balance formal details showcasing your passion and personality. Keep it simple and avoid technical jargon. You want people reading your business plan to understand your vision. Ask a friend to read and give feedback so that you can make necessary changes to make your proposal valuable for all.

A visual representation of graphs, charts and images conveys the message better than tables with numbers so include relevant images in your plan.

Use standard formatting in the document with the right font, page numbering, sizes of headings, branding and logo.

Think about a presentation. You can in fact create a PowerPoint presentation about your business plan.

Bank Loan Guide:

Fund is the major factor standing between the success and failure of a start-up.

If government grants and crowd funding sources are not available, you can approach banks and apply for funding capital through a business loan. This will be nerve-wracking. Banks do lend money easily, they are selective. You need to put together a loan application that will convince the bank to fund your business venture.

The Application Guide:

Research all funding possibilities. You do not have to depend only on a bank for a loan. Search and shop around for funding opportunities including venture capitalists.

Make sure your loan application also includes your business plan that shows how you intend to earn profit as well as how the cash flow will assist the way forward.

Make sure all documentation is in order and do check your credit rating as well. Be prepared for the loan interview process with bank or lending organisation officials by researching possible questions. It is best to prepare beforehand so that you are not caught off guard during the interview session.

Practice Your Pitch:

Practice the pitch that you are going to make to your prospective financier so it does not sound scripted. Try to learn facts, points, aim to be fluent and do not just memorise the points. Make it a personal approach. Go to the bank or funding agency in person to seek a special meeting. Above all cross check to see if your application is realistic.

Do not underestimate your funding requirement, which may result in you approaching the funding agency again for additional finances. Such an approach will not make a good impression. Do not undervalue your costs and include honest figures for the entire business process.

Worksheet:

An entrepreneur exploring a potential new venture must ask if the concept will earn a profit.

This is where a worksheet will help answer questions and transform an idea into a successfully functioning business.

What are the main points to review when analysing if your concept is feasible?

Your worksheet will help you arrive at a comprehensive plan. A worksheet is a recording system that gathers and analyses information related to the success of your new venture.

It is a screening process to identify business opportunities that a business plan should be developed around.

It is also a feasibility study the includes, a preliminary assessment, defines the concept of the new venture, presents a marketing assessment, includes a cost analysis to determine profit and evolves future action plans.

This worksheet will assess the feasibility of the concept that you have. It helps to screen out concepts that are limited by opportunity and allows investment of time, effort and money into ideas that have a high potential.

Preliminary Assessment:

This step evaluates and chooses the venture, assessing potential and profit generating ability in a time frame that factors in both project and personal considerations.

Before evaluating the financial feasibility of the business idea ask yourself; Why did you initiate the concept? What do you want to accomplish by starting the venture?

Define: Your short-term goals in the first year; intermediate goals (1–3 years); long-term (3–5 years).

Personal Considerations:

It is important to get your family's reaction on your proposed business venture and how the venture will affect them.

You will also have to give thought to how your personal and family lifestyle will be altered when you launch your own business venture.

Another area to consider is do you have the required skill set to deliver or do you need to hire people to make up for the skills you lack?

The Concept:

Once personal evaluation and family commitment have been identified as well as the ability to carry out the venture is on hand, the next step is to analyse the potential success the business venture can bring. It is critical to explain clearly and concisely what your products or services are. An idea that is well defined will ensure that the feasibility of the venture is accurate and contains information that is required to make a decision that is well informed.

Describe the business you seek to enter and list services or products that you wish to sell: also list those who will most likely use your products or services.

Market Assessment:

A critical component of any business is assessing the market potential of a new venture. A miscalculation that many entrepreneurs make is measuring the appeal of their product based on their personal or family appeal. They assume consumers will be drawn to a product like their family members and purchase the product. What is needed is an unbiased and comprehensive analysis of the product. This will assist in determining the true viability of the idea or venture. With proper market research you can refine the product based on valuable information gathered about the industry, market size, customers, competition and customer profiles.

There is a need for a thorough understanding of potential customers. This is essential to achieve success. When you define who customers are, you describe them in broad terms as individuals who have the need for your service or product.

This gives the impression of the larger market or the niche market that you are proposing to target. The success of the venture depends on the ability to meet the needs of customers and the target market must be clearly defined.

Describe who your potential customers are? Where are they based? What are specific tastes and needs they have? What are they able to afford?

Demographic Description:

Every customer is unique, but as a whole they are categorised into groups. This ranges from income, lifestyles and characteristics. People in a certain group may choose a product as it meets their specific needs.

The demographic information provides meaningful insight that relates the interest of potential customers, their ability and needs to purchase services or products you have on offer.

These are the key points to identify in order to define demographic profiles of the potential target market.

Geographic Description:

Define the geographic area that you intend to market your services or products. This definition needs to be specific and indicate whether the venture will serve a specific city, region, country or province. It is also important to look at the density of the population.

DEFINING THE GEOGRAPHIC PROFILE OF THE TARGET MARKET

Psychological factors examine self-image aspects and this defines what the customers see or what they want to see.

Characteristic Traits of Target Customers:

- Trendsetting
- Status seeking
- Conservative
- Environmentally conscious
- Family oriented
- Other

Purchasing Description:

- Identify purchasing patterns of target consumers. This can predict sales trends.
- Will they purchase the service or product?
- How often will they purchase the product?
- How much will they purchase?
- How will they continue to make use of the service or product?
- Where will they be able to buy the product?

Assess the size of the market and evaluate trends that may affect buying habits.

And the market size: Identify if the customer base is large enough in order to be able to sustain the venture. Determine if the market is sufficient in size. The geographic and demographic information will be able to assist in this assessment.

Trends:

- Identify market trends that can affect your targeted market in the future and it is equally important to assess the potential of the new market which the new venture you intend to undertake.

- This will determine the viability of the company in the long-term, the opportunities that are present and how to respond to changing behaviours.

Define the Size of the Current Market:
- Define the customer base growth.
- Define changes taking place within the target market.
- Define the changes that affect customer's ability and desire.
- Define the changes taking place that will affect customers' ability and desire to purchase your product or service.

Industry Analysis:

Every venture is unique, but all business is part of a larger industry and forces affecting that specific industry will impact on the business. To be successful there is a need to plan and recognise issues that may affect the new venture.

Describe the industry:
- Describe trends in the industry.
- Describe opportunities in the industry.
- Describe the category of under which your business or industry will fall.
- Describe the size of that industry.
- Describe the potential growth of that industry?
- Describe what regulation will affect that particular industry and how those regulations will impact your venture?
- Describe opportunities that can be identified in the industry?

Competition:

Analysing competition is a fundamental in market research. You need the information in order to determine what your market potential will be.

Direct Competition: This occurs between marketers of the same products.

Indirect Competition: These are marketers of similar products.

Define Your Competitors:

- What are the strengths of the competitor?
- What are the weaknesses of the competitor?
- What is the quality of service provided by the competitor?
- What is the price being offered by the competitor?
- What customers do they tend to attract?
- What defines their success?
- What makes the product or service you offer unique?
- Why could customers purchase your service and product rather than the competitor's?

If the feasibility study indicates that the venture is not deemed to be profitable, do not be disappointed. Be grateful that time, effort and capital have been saved for a new possible concept that might materialise.

INTROSPECTION QUESTIONNAIRE

1. What are the basic things that you need to follow while starting up a business?

   _____
   _____

2. What are the systems to be considered for starting a new business?

   _____
   _____

3. How will you manage the cash flow and what are the precautionary measures that you would take to run a smooth business?

   _____
   _____

4. Why should you write a business plan prior to starting a new business?

   _____

   _____

5. How will you do a business analysis to determine the profit?

   _____

   _____

Chapter – 3

*"Quality in a service or product is not what you put into it;
It is what the customer gets out of it"*

Production and Quality Assurance

1. Process / Objectives / Fundamentals / Stages

2. Benefits of Improving Production Planning

3. Effective Production Management Strategy

4. Reduce your business waste to save money

5. Research & Development

6. Effective Procurement Fundamentals

> ### Abhishek Mohan Gupta – Higher Education Mission:
>
> Family business was always a priority for Abhishek Mohan Gupta even when he was studying for his graduation.
>
> Passionate about helping people, he joined his father's not-for-profit organisation Jagran Social Welfare Society which runs 4 branches of Delhi Public Schools in Bhopal and Indore under the aegis of the Delhi Public School Society, New Delhi as well as Jagran Lakecity University. The society provides quality education to more than 35,000 students.
>
> Abhishek embarked on globalisation and digitalisation focussing on diversity with brand building as the key for success.
>
> With support from mentors and his father, he was made in-charge of higher education and spearheaded its growth. It was a huge responsibility and Abhishek had to overcome many hurdles.
>
> As the proverb goes, his failure became a stepping stone for success. While his first venture at higher education had to shut down, his single-minded dedication resulted in the launching of a private university in 2013, which has been awarded as the best private university for 3 years in succession. Gupta now reigns among the top 50 influential leaders of Asia.

Product planning is a process of discussing and defining features of a product before its development. There are a number of phases to product planning, including gathering input, refining ideas, approving and designating projects and tasks, refining market requirements and beginning product development. Product planning is important for a number of reasons. Product planning is a plan for the future production, in which facilities or inputs needed are determined and arranged. A product plan is made periodically over a specific time period, called as planning horizon. It can comprise the following activities:

- Determination of the required product blend and factory load to satisfy customer needs.
- Matching the required level of production to the existing resources.
- Scheduling and choosing the actual work to be started in the manufacturing facility.

- Setting up and delivering production orders to production facilities.

- In order to develop a practical production plan, the product planner or product planning department needs to work closely with the marketing department and sales department. They can provide sales forecasts or a listing of customers' orders. The work is usually selected from a variety of product types which may require different resources and serve different customers.

- Therefore, the selection must optimise customer-independent performance measures such as cycle time and customer-dependent performance measures such as on time delivery.

A critical factor in product planning is the accurate estimation of production capacity of available resources; this is one of the most difficult tasks to perform. Product planning should always take into account material availability, resource availability and knowledge of future demand.

PROCESS OF PRODUCT PLANNING

Pay Attention to Everyone's Views and Opinions:

One of the earliest stages of product planning is gathering inputs about a new product idea. This step is important because it allows you to step back and look at ideas from a number of different groups of people, including your developers, sales team, customer support team, shareholders, management and your customers. All perspectives are important, but pay close attention to customer feedback. You can conduct a survey to ask existing customers about features they want and price they would pay, as well as any other details specific to your product. This also gives everyone involved a chance to weigh in so no one feels like their idea was not acknowledged.

Assess and Examine Ideas:

In most of the cases, there are a lot of ideas about a new product. While some may be conflicting, others may be unrealistic and some just miss the mark and do not work at all, so you will need to evaluate and sort through all ideas to find the best. Document and discuss each idea with your product marketing team. If one or more ideas for the product pop up multiple times, chances are that it is an idea worth pursuing. It is important to acknowledge all ideas and evaluate which ones are the best, then refine those ideas to include specific details about a product, such as features. These refined ideas are the initial plan or design for the product.

Investigate the Market Segment:

Another part of product planning is analysing the market. Specifically, you must look at the latest consumer trends and behaviour in your proposed new industry/business or market. Pay attention to what similar products are selling best, what features or product details consumers are attracted to, and what are they spending on for other similar products. Make note of features or functionality that are missing from similar products but are wanted or needed by your target customers. This information is important because it allows you to make changes to the product before production begins, as well as helping you begin to think about how to successfully market the product to drive sales.

Ascertain Cycle of New Product and Existing Product:

Product planning also helps you establish a time line for the cycle of a new product, from conception to design and production. A time line is important to give you a target launch date. However, be cautious when establishing deadlines; do not be too aggressive, or else you might set your team up for failure.

Ordering Materials:

Materials and services that require a long lead time or are at an extended shipping distance, also known as blanket orders, should be ordered in advance of production requirements. Suppliers should send you materials periodically to ensure an uninterrupted pipeline.

Procurement of Equipment:

Procuring specialised tools and equipment to initiate the production process may require a longer lead time. Keep in mind that the equipment may have to be custom made or simply difficult to set-up. This type of equipment may also require special training.

Identify Potential Constraints:

These are constraints or restrictions in the process flow and this should be identified in advance so you can plan around them or eliminate them before you begin the production process. When you identify possible bottlenecks, be aware that they may shift to another area of the process. Dealing with bottlenecks is a continual challenge for any business.

Human Resources Recruitment and Training:

Key or specialised positions may demand extensive training on specialised equipment, technical processes or regulatory requirements. Candidates for such positions should be interviewed thoroughly about their skills. When hiring them, allow sufficient time for training and be sure that they are competent in their work before the job begins. This will ensure that your process or service flows smoothly.

Make Teams Aware of Your Plan:

After you have determined that you have met the criteria to start production, you will need to communicate the plan to the employees who will implement it. You can plan the production on spreadsheets, databases or software, which usually speeds the process up. However, a visual representation is preferred as a means to communicate operation schedules to floor employees. Some businesses post work orders on boards or use computer monitors to display the floor schedule. The schedule also needs to be available to employees ahead of time and needs to be kept up to date.

Factor in Future and Immediate Change:

One of the many challenges of product planning and scheduling is following-up with changes to orders. Changes happen every day, you will need to adjust your plan in line with these changes and advise the production unit suitably. Dealing with change is not always easy and may take as much effort as creating the original production plan. You will need to follow-up with the various departments involved in order to rectify any problems. Computer software can be helpful in tracking changes, inventory, employees and equipment.

Production planning and control is a predetermined process which includes optimal use of human resources, raw materials and machines. Production planning is the technique to plan each and every step in a long series of separate operations. It helps to take the right decision at the right time and at the right place to achieve maximum efficiency.

Objectives of Production Planning:

- Ensuring safe and economical production process.
- Effective utilisation of the plant to maximise productivity.
- To maximise efficiency by proper coordination in production process.
- To ensure proper delivery of goods.
- To place the right man for the right job, at right time for right wages.
- To minimise labour turnover.
- To reduce waiting time.

FOLLOWING ARE THE FUNDAMENTALS OF PRODUCTION PLANNING

- Routing
- Loading
- Scheduling
- Dispatching
- Follow-up
- Inspection
- Corrective

Routing: It is about selection of path or route through which raw materials pass in order to convert them into a finished product. The points to be noted while routing process are – full capacity of machines, economical and short route as well as availability of alternate routing. Setting up time for the process for each stage of route needs to be fixed. Once overall sequence is fixed, the standard time of operations is noted using work measurement technique.

Loading and Scheduling: Loading and scheduling are concerned with preparation of workloads and fixing of starting and completing dates for each operation in the manufacturing industry. On the basis of the performance of each machine, loading and scheduling tasks are completed.

Dispatching: Dispatching is the process of ensuring that the production goes as per plan with proper assignment of raw materials based on equipment and staff capacity to meet the demands as scheduled in advance, in short a process to ensure smooth work flow of production activities to meet targeted requirements with interventions if required when there are some hitches.

Expediting: It is a control tool which brings an idea on breaking up delay and rectifying flaws during the progress of work.

Inspection: Inspection is to find out the quality of executed work process.

Corrective: At evaluation process, a thorough analysis is done and corrective measures are taken to rectify weak spots.

Stages of Production Planning:

Production planning is a 3-stage process as indicated below, this may not apply to all types of production processes but it is applicable to most cases:

- Pre-planning
- Planning
- Control

Pre-Planning: In this phase of production planning, basic ground work on the product design, layout design and work flow are prepared. The operations relating to the availability scope and capacity of human resources, funds, materials, machines and time frame for launching business are estimated.

Planning: This is a phase where a complete analysis on routing, estimating and scheduling is done. It also tries to find out areas of concern in the short-term and long-term so that appropriate action plans can be prepared.

Control: In this phase, functions included are dispatching, follow-up, inspection and evaluation. This phase tries to analyse and expedite the work in progress. This is one of the important phases of the production planning and control.

Benefits of Improving Production Planning:

Production planning and inventory control sounds complicated, but when done correctly, it does provide many opportunities to reduce cost and increase productivity. Advances in computer technology and software also make a lot of the computation easier. It is important to learn fundamentals well and let Excel deal with the mathematics portion of the planning process. Production planning and inventory control can be defined as the process of planning the production in advance, setting exact route map for each item, fixing starting and finishing dates for each item, giving production orders to shops and following-up progress of products based on orders. It also involves ensuring the availability of the right quantity of raw materials or components while avoiding overstocking or running out of stock. To maximise productivity, every company needs a sound production plan. However, effective planning is a complex process that covers a wide variety of activities to ensure that materials, equipment and human resources are available when and where they are needed. Production planning is like a roadmap: It helps you know where you are going and how long it will take for you to get there.

Advantages of An Effective Production Planning:

Capacity planning helps you have just the right amount of equipment, labour and supplies for your target production capacity. The following are the merits of an effective production plan:

- Reduce your inventory costs by decreasing the need for safety stocks and excessive work-in-process inventories.

- Reduce your labour costs by eliminating wastage time and improving process flow.

- Optimise equipment usage and increased capacity and improve your return on assets.

- Make your customers happy with improved on time deliveries of products and services.

Steps to An Effective Production Management Strategy:

Overcoming challenges of making a company expand manufacturing operations to make it more customer driven needs to start with a clear definition of what success means.

Having accurate, real-time production visibility improves product quality, order accuracy and customer satisfaction while pushing down manufacturing costs at the plant level.

Keeping manufacturing operations across all locations focussed on a common set of goals improves gross margins, reducing the total cost per unit while improving on time order delivery and perfect order performance.

The era of manufacturing intelligence has arrived, fuelled by data from manufacturing execution systems with manufacturing operations management strategies accelerating adoption company-wide.

Improving product quality, reducing cycle times, automating manual workflows and streamlining plant floor operations are a few of the many benefits of adopting a company-wide manufacturing operations management strategy.

Defining the strategic goal of having all production centres contributing to a series of company-wide lean manufacturing, supply chain, quality, and production, service and customer satisfaction goals galvanises diverse production locations together.

Instead of having to rely on many different, disconnected systems to manage diverse production locations to a common set of goals, manufacturers are adopting company-wide manufacturing execution management systems.

Planning and scheduling, quality management, inventory optimisation, tooling management, preventive and predictive maintenance, and manufacturing intelligence are the core functional areas included in manufacturing execution system (MES) today.

Meeting Customer Expectations of Real-Time Responsiveness and Quality:

Across all selling and service channels customers expect real-time responses to their questions in addition to product quality that is world class. How well a manufacturer meets or exceeds these expectations will have a big impact on their future growth opportunities. This is the reason is why having a scalable, secure manufacturing operations management strategy in place is key to future growth.

The core components of this strategy are available in an MES. They need to be orchestrated to excel in the context of a given manufacturer's unique challenges. While each manufacturer's operations strategies and challenges are different, many share the following:

- Increasing company-wide production efficiency across all plant locations from the production team to the location level while reducing costs.
- Making quality a core part of production operations with each plant making contributions to overarching quality goals instead of allowing it to be a function.
- Achieving real-time supply chain, order management and production performance visibility across all manufacturing operations.
- Excelling at data collection of the machine, team and plant level, including piloting Internet of Things as a means to capture data in real-time.
- Defining manufacturing operations analytics that encompasses all production centres and provides updates on overall equipment effectiveness (OEE) and manufacturing intelligence.

Waste is an increasing problem for businesses as disposal costs increase, tighter legislation is imposed and it becomes more difficult to find facilities that accept waste. By analysing the causes of waste within your business processes and taking a systematic approach to eliminating them, you can keep your business waste disposal problems to a minimum. Lean Thinking and Six Sigma are business management techniques that can help streamline workflow, deliver quality improvements, increase efficiency and profitability in all forms of businesses. Reducing waste and becoming more efficient often go hand in hand. However, there are times when you may need to decide between reducing the amount of waste you generate and making your processes more efficient.

Reduce Your Business Waste to Save Money:

Reduce waste in production: Waste arising in production processes can have a significant effect on profitability. The challenge is to reduce waste from production without undermining the effectiveness of the process. Some typical problems include the excessive consumption of energy or raw materials, losses in the production process itself, rejection at the inspection stage and failure when the customer is using the end product. To know where waste is arising, you need to have a detailed understanding of the process. You can get a production manager to produce a flowchart of the operation. You can then discuss the process with other relevant employees and get their feedback on where waste is occurring and what you could do to reduce it. This broad-brush approach helps you focus on the most important areas with more detailed analysis following later if necessary. Common things you might do to improve the efficiency of production processes and reduce waste include:

- Reusing rinsed water in cooling systems.
- Regularly checking that equipment is correctly calibrated.
- Reducing unnecessary stoppages in a production line.
- Upgrading or replacing old equipment.
- Minimising spills or leaks.
- Using sealed systems.

Prevention is better than cure, of course. Constant monitoring of your production processes and preventive maintenance can ensure waste is avoided before it occurs.

RESEARCH AND DEVELOPMENT

How to Forecast Production In Your Seasonal Business:

The following definition of forecast uncertainties is based on the Physical Resources Management System definition of resource uncertainty, but broadens it to also address forecast uncertainties in the short and medium term, thus the whole time line. This forecast definition will enable a lean forecasting process by allowing for a single, consistent forecast that will be the basis for resource estimation, decision making and business planning. The basic principle is that for any given project and subproject, there is a forecast and an uncertainty range that describes the imperfections in the input data and fully captures the current risks and up sides of the forecast.

Forecast uncertainty ranges may be derived probabilistically or by deterministic scenarios, but they must always cover both the long-term and short-term uncertainties.

The low case forecast therefore combines the low case in ultimate recovery or remaining reserves with a low case in project delivery and system availability. The "consistent model" could be a simulation model or IPSM (integrated production system model), but it could also be a decline curve or proxy model that combines the near-term uncertainty with the low case for ultimate recovery.

Making the best estimate forecast with an IPSM and the low case with a decline curve model could still be considered a "consistent model" if properly justified; however, making the first 2 years with a decline curve model and the out years with an IPSM would not be considered a consistent model.

Forecasting methods, such as decline curve analysis, type curve analysis, material balance, analogue methods, simulation models and IPSM.

How to establish forecast input uncertainty, with respect to subsurface, activity scheduling and system constraints.

Principles:

At any point in time, there is only one best estimate forecast for a project that reflects the current understanding of subsurface uncertainty and best development and commercial assumptions. This forecast should always be accompanied by an uncertainty range.

The forecast uncertainty range should always have remaining reserves or EUR as an objective function. The forecast and uncertainty range should be based on defined projects, with incremental forecasts for subsequent projects.

With these principles, forecasting is part of asset management throughout the financial year. It may be envisaged as a continuous loop through the whole upstream lifecycle. Forecast updates are triggered by reserves and corporate planning, but also by ad hoc changes and events, such as studies and subsurface information and development plan updates. For official forecast of reserves and corporate planning, reasonable freeze dates should be agreed upon for input data and should be adhered to. The forecast model is kept up to date and consistent with the latest surveillance data and development assumptions and when reserves or corporate forecast need to be updated, it may simply be derived from the latest model.

Always Update Customer Terms and Conditions:

Discounts should be planned far ahead of time: There are 2 primary types of discounts a retailer might give customers; Promotional discounts during season and clearance discounts as the season winds down. Planning these discounts goes hand in hand with planning sales and inventories if you are using retail value as your unit of measure. A discount, just like a sale, decreases the retail value of your inventory on hand. Keep in mind that any retailer needs to protect gross margins and cash flow when planning clearance discounts. If you plan the date of the first seasonal discount even before the season begins, you can plan the inventory you want to have on hand at that point in time. If you have planned sales by month, ending inventories by month, and discounts by month, it's easy to calculate how much inventory to bring in each month, by category.

Retailers need to bring in enough to cover that month's planned sales, planned discounts, and planned ending inventory, minus the prior month's planned ending inventory. Throughout history, advances in technology have allowed people to pursue creativity and expand their minds to develop even more technological advancements. As technology advances, so does productivity, increasing the capacity for future technological advances. In the business world, these technological advances, creative pursuits, and increased productivity translate into higher profits. Application of these concepts: technology, creativity, and productivity can and should be applied to every facet of your business so that you can be as effective and efficient as possible.

Effective Procurement Fundamentals Include the Following:

- Developing fundamental capabilities
- Bringing accountability throughout your organisation
- Embracing innovation

Having a sound procurement strategy allows companies to survive economic downturns by applying cost-cutting measures when necessary and to adjust appropriately when the situation changes. Being able to deliver on all 3 qualities is what separates high performing from weak performing procurement organisations.

Increasing Fundamental Capabilities:

Without the necessary foundation and base level understanding of what your organisation needs, a procurement strategy will not be effective. Being capable of delivering basic procurement is the first step towards increasing efficiencies. Many companies are stuck trying to get through their procurement process by focussing only on improving fundamental capabilities. The problem with merely getting by is that unless something changes, your situation won't improve. Companies can get stuck muddling on with an ad hoc solution for years not realising that there are more effective alternatives. Most companies focus on developing their basic functions for a few key staff members without successfully implementing organisation wide adoption.

Expand Your Resource Base:

Procurement is most effective when roles of users, suppliers and management are aligned with the strategic direction of an organisation. A Chief Procurement Officer (CPO) should foster an environment where procurement policies are adopted throughout an organisation to develop spends saving and cost effective results to an organisation. A strong strategic leader will be able to influence their company and enable forward strategic thinking. Ensure your whole organisation is trained to use your procurement process as this can reduce or even eliminate maverick spending and will increase spend visibility. While the set-up, monitoring and implementation of a system should be left to the procurement team, the purchasing process should be simplified and distributed throughout the organisation. An influential leader will understand the importance of strategic adoption but what separates a great leader is their casino desire to embrace innovation. Ask your staff for feedback. Find out where road blocks or gaps in knowledge are as it's easier to get staff buy in when they feel genuinely included in the process.

Embrace Innovation:

By combining fundamental capabilities, organisation wide adoption and innovation, companies are able to outpace their peers. Procurement relies on the ever changing marketplace and without embracing innovation companies can easily lose their competitive edge. Procurement has the opportunity to delve into buying patterns, consumer tendencies, vendor preferences, contract negotiation, and a wealth of relevant data. Organisations that capitalise on data and absorb the metrics into their strategic planning are often times much more prepared when dealing with changes in the market. They are more willing to adopt new technology, have a company culture ready to adopt policy change, and have more than basic capabilities and are in a position to develop advanced, forward thinking strategies. Effective procurement combines base level skill with company influence while embracing innovation. It can seem like a monumental task to evolve your organisation but radical change usually starts with one small step.

Focussing On Solving Inaccuracies and Administration:

Global competition, faster product development, increasingly flexible manufacturing systems and an unprecedented number as well as variety of products are competing in markets ranging from apparel and toys to power tools and computers. Instead of being beneficial to consumers, this phenomenon is making it more difficult for manufacturers and retailers to predict which of their goods will sell and to plan production and orders accordingly. As a result, inaccurate forecasts are increasing, and along with them costs of those errors. Manufacturers and retailers alike are ending up with more unwanted goods that must be marked down perhaps even sold at a loss even as they lose potential sales because other articles are no longer in stock. In industries with highly volatile demand, like fashion apparel, the costs of such "stock outs" and markdowns can actually exceed the total cost of manufacturing.

To address the problem of inaccurate forecasts, many managers have turned to one or another popular production-scheduling system. But quick response programmes, just-in-time (JIT) inventory systems, manufacturing resource planning and the like are simply not up to the task. With a tool like manufacturing resource planning, for example, a manufacturer can rapidly change the production schedule stored on a computer when original forecasts and plans prove incorrect. Creating a new schedule doesn't help, though, if the supply chain has already been stocked up based on the previous schedule or plan.

Similarly, quick response and JIT address only part of the overall picture. A manufacturer might hope to be fast enough to produce in direct response to demand, virtually eliminating the need for a forecast. But in many industries, sales of volatile products tend to occur in a concentrated season, which means that a manufacturer would need an unjustifiably large capacity to be able to make goods in response to actual demand. Using quick response or JIT also may not be feasible if a company is dependent on an unresponsive supplier for key components. We think that manufacturers and retailers alike can greatly reduce the cost of forecasting errors by embracing accurate response, a new approach to the entire forecasting, planning, and production process. We believe that companies can improve their forecasts and simultaneously redesign their planning processes to minimise the impact of inaccurate forecasts. Accurate response provides a way to do both. It entails figuring out what forecasters can and cannot predict well, and then making the supply chain fast and flexible so that managers can postpone decisions about their most unpredictable items until they have some market signals, such as early-season sales results, to help correctly match supply with demand.

Accurate response helps retailers improve forecasts and redesign planning processes to minimise the impact of inaccurate forecasts. This approach incorporates 2 basic elements that other forecasting and scheduling systems either totally or partially lack. First, it takes into account missed sales opportunities. Forecasting errors result in too little or too much inventory. Accurate response measures the costs per unit of stock outs and markdowns, and factors them into the planning process. Most companies do not even measure how many sales they have lost, let alone consider those costs when they commit to production.

A key factor behind business success is ensuring efficient production planning and control, which will allow your high product quality to stand out from the rest, despite high cost pressure and intensifying competition. For order-related production in particular, as well as long-term planning, the ability to react flexibly in the short-term is also important.

INTROSPECTION QUESTIONNAIRE

1. Define the process of production planning.

_____

_____

2. Why should you revisit your production plan periodically?

3. How will you avoid production waste? What are the cost saving areas to focus on to increase your profit margin?

4. What is production forecast?

5. What are fundamentals of effective procurement?

Chapter – 4

*"Good Marketing makes the Company look smart;
Great Marketing makes the Customer feel smart"*

Marketing & Sales

- Sales & Marketing - Responsibilities & Techniques
- Material Handling & Warehousing
- Market Research
- Distribution Channels
- Return on Investment (ROI)
- Developing a Sales strategy
- Improving customer service

Santosh Kumar – Paris de Salon:

An entrepreneur who breathes versatility, he comes from a family that has been in the textiles business for 4 decades and he has ventured into multiple businesses. He runs an esteem jewellery furnishings and a niche salon brand set-up in the year 2010.

Coming from a background of modelling, he has endeavoured into the wellness space. Modelling was his passion but it was not a career path for him. He set of into diverse businesses with the idea of not needing to depend on single business at recession times.

Eyeing the glamour industry of Bollywood and VIP clan of politicians, he established the high-end salon business with 2 exclusive centres. His business logic was that hair care, facial care, body care and skin care was a never ending business.

He has an elite customer base and ensures that they have their maximum privacy. His salon business has now become more of a passion for him than a brand.

In summary, business networking can have a significant positive impact on your sales success. It can also be a big time waster. Be prepared, be special, be in the right places, and help others. Do these things and you become someone well respected in the business community! Is having a great product the only requirement to run a successful business? For most companies, the answer is no. Why? Because generating sales requires potential customers to understand that a product exists, what it does, and why it's better than a competitor's offering. The responsibility to communicate that information rests on the shoulders of the marketing and sales teams. Typically, marketing has a predominant role at the beginning of a potential sale. For instance, a marketing team may develop a new radio campaign to help spread awareness about a product launch. A sales team works to finalise a deal by communicating directly with leads and addressing their concerns. Another advantage sales and marketing teams exploit, is collaboration. Rather than operating as independent units, strong information and idea sharing between the teams can help improve results and create a seamless experience for prospective buyers. Here's a comprehensive overview of the meaning, responsibilities, and techniques of each segment.

Defining Sales and Marketing:

Sales include operations and activities involved in promoting and selling products or services with the main objective of customer satisfaction through provision of goods and services at the right time and place.

Marketing includes the technique of promoting, selling, and distributing a product or service. These statements highlight 2 aspects of the sales and marketing relationship, they are also the main objectives of marketing. The responsibilities of each group are closely linked. Marketing has a vital role in supporting sales.

In practice, the marketing department tends to bear responsibility for raising awareness about a product and generating high-quality leads for a sales team. A marketing-qualified lead is a lead that meets certain criteria set forth by a marketing department. A sales-qualified lead adds to the initial stipulations set forth by marketing to help find the highest value prospects. At times, a sales department may complain that marketing leads do not meet the standard set forth by the sales team. However, the potential for conflict also represents an opportunity for collaboration. The more effectively the 2 teams can share ideas, the better aligned their definitions are likely to be.

Sales and Marketing Responsibilities:

While sometimes grouped separately, sales and marketing functions overlap. Those businesses that recognise the critical areas of overlap may get more value out of their teams by combining efforts. After all, both sales and marketing have the same end goal: increasing sales.

Sales Responsibilities:

Following-Up: A key sales function is following-up with the leads generated by a marketing department. Successful businesses usually develop a structured handoff process so that each marketing-qualified lead receives appropriate and timely follow-up from a sales team member.

Building Long-Lasting Relationships: The era of the "hard sell" continues to fade. Modern sales focus on relationship building to help create trust between a buyer and seller. Effective salespersons can understand the needs of the buyer and develop a persuasive but not pushy message to help differentiate the company's product.

Closing: Most salespersons are judged by their ability to turn leads into customers. While some may envision a face-to-face meeting and handshake as the close of a sale, many businesses also close sales online or over the phone. This can broaden the responsibilities of closing a sale to more employees.

Customer Retention: Sales and marketing have responsibility for improving client retention. By checking in with an existing client, a sales team member can help demonstrate an interest in long-term client success, not just a one-time sale. The ongoing effort to build strong relationships can help improve retention and lead to additionally increase sales beyond the initial purchase.

Responsibilities of Marketing:

Create Awareness: An effort to build awareness of a product or service is the first step in the sales process. A successful awareness-building effort may help a prospective buyer recognise a brand or product name or may ensure a company makes the shortlist for purchasing consideration.

Deepen Customer and Market Engagement: These efforts build on an initial awareness campaign to deepen a consumer's connection to a company or product. Marketing materials aimed at engagement may be longer compared to a more superficial awareness piece for instance, a direct mail or radio advertisement.

Conversion: A conversion is the critical transition of a potential customer from an anonymous person to a known lead. For marketing teams, a conversion may be the completion of a web form, the instigation of a web chat, or a phone call to a customer service line.

Customer Retention: Even after a purchase, a marketing team can help a business grow its repeat customers. The retention function of marketing helps maintain awareness and engagement after a sale. This may include email newsletters or invitations to seminars that help a consumer get more value from a product. The retention function of marketing is especially critical for subscription services.

Role of Technology: Today's technology has a key role in sales and marketing. It also has a role in facilitating collaboration between the

2 business units. A prominent example of sales and marketing technology is the Customer Relationship Management (CRM) system. A CRM serves as a single resource with all client information. This information can help sales teams better understand how a customer became a lead. For instance, a CRM may contain information about the source of a lead, such as a trade show or TV ad. From a marketing perspective, a CRM can help track leads throughout the sales cycle. This information can provide valuable feedback to marketing teams about which marketing channels generate the most sales-qualified leads, actual sales, or longest client retention.

Sales and Marketing Techniques:

How do sales and marketing teams achieve their goals? The tactics vary based on the industry and company culture. They have also changed over time. These are some of the common sales and marketing techniques that form the core of each practice.

Sales Techniques:

Limiting the Offer or Product Version and After Sales' Service Opportunity: The idea of a "limited-time offer" is common in retail, but creating a sense of scarcity is a tactic used in many industries. A limited opportunity may be limited by time for instance an offer is good for a particular month only or during its stock availability.

Concentrating On Pain Points: An effective salesperson can frame benefits of a product or service regarding the needs of a client. This means understanding the day-to-day challenges a client faces and focussing on how a product can solve those issues. An emphasis on pain points can also help build a relationship by showing a salesperson's interest in a customer's problem.

Making An Assumptive Close: The assumptive close is a sales technique that changes a request for a "yes" into a "no." For instance, rather than asking, "Do you want to try this service?" a salesperson may instead ask, "When would you like us to schedule the installation?"

Outbound Marketing: Outbound marketing represents traditional "push" marketing. This includes television advertisements, direct mail flyers, and cold calling. Outbound marketing tactics often are effective in generating broad awareness among particular demography. However, some modern marketing strategies question the ability of outbound marketing to develop persuasive, personal marketing messages that build lasting company – customer relationships.

Inbound Marketing: Inbound marketing shifts marketing efforts from "push" to "pull." The core idea behind inbound marketing is to draw potential customers in by creating marketing materials that help consumers. For example, an investment firm may offer a free seminar on retirement planning. Inbound marketing tends to focus first on providing a consumer with something valuable, rather than maintaining an inward focus on delivering a company message.

Therefore, technology can help sales and marketing teams:

- Identify the most successful tactics.
- Make it easier for teams to align best practices.

The analytics provided by a CRM can help identify each touch point throughout the marketing and sales process that is critical to a sale. That information, in turn, can provide a data-backed rationale for adjusting techniques employed in each process. Further, the modern CRM and supporting technologies may make it easier for sales and marketing teams to implement techniques that work best. This could include automating the distribution of marketing materials or streamlining the handoff process between teams. Technology such as computer telephony integration (CTI) can even help teams handle "unplanned" handoffs, like when a prospect calls a customer service line instead of their dedicated sales representative. CTI integration can help manage real-time access to customer data in a CRM and route calls efficiently to the most qualified representative.

How to Improve the Sales and Marketing Department:

The effort to improve the sales and marketing department is ongoing. However, it begins with an understanding of the role of each service so that a business can establish clear and reasonable goals. From there, the development of each department depends on the identification of the right tactics, which vary based on how a business prefers to interact with its customers. Along the way, technology can help organise the process and make it more efficient. It can also play a role in improving information sharing between the 2 departments, which may help each reach their shared goals of more sales and a thriving business.

When thinking about how business networking fits within your overall marketing plans, ask yourself these questions:

- How many people do you want to meet?
- How many leads do you want to generate?
- How much of your sales plan do you want to achieve via business networking?

Knowing answers to these questions will enable you to determine how much time and exactly what kinds of networking activities and events in which you should be involved. Beyond setting your goals, here are 5 proven methods that should be an important part of your networking marketing plan.

Network In A Target Rich Environment & Stand Out from the Crowd: Know who and what kinds of people you want to meet and find the organisations and activities in which they are involved. Don't go to networking events unless that's where your target market is. Otherwise, you are sub-optimising your time. Do not just be among the crowd; get involved in the organisation as a volunteer. Seek a leadership position. Become known as someone more important and involved than the other hundreds or so people that participates in an organisation. If you don't stand out and don't have a competitive advantage, try something different because business networking may not be the right thing for you.

Help Others and You Will Be Helping Yourself: The old saying "givers gain" means you first should give and then you'll gain from that giving. Call it "the right thing to do" or karma, but this old adage holds true in business networking. Focus first on how you can help others make the connections they want to make. When you meet someone, ask him/her, "Who are you looking to meet?" or "What kinds of businesses do you want to connect to?" You'll become known as a master networker, people will seek you out and you'll enhance your personal and your company's brand.

Be Prepared to Pitch With An Open-Ended Question: Get your marketing elevator pitch or unique selling proposition (USP) ready so it rolls off your tongue as easily as your name. When someone asks what you do, you want to articulate your USP with confidence and ease which is very important. Be ready with a good open-ended question when you meet someone. A question like "Who are you looking to meet?" or "What does your firm do and how might I be able to help you meet the people you are seeking?" Questions like these will get the other person talking and communicate that you want to help them.

Follow-Up After Meeting: If you connect with someone good, follow-up with a kind email or handwritten note expressing gratitude for his/her time. It will make you memorable. Humility and gratitude are traits of every successful sales and marketing professional. Don't just add the person to your email database so they begin getting your unsolicited emails. Instead, in your follow email or note saying that you will include them in your newsletters and hope he/she finds them valuable but don't hesitate to unsubscribe if you don't. Seek feedback and advice about your information, that's a sign that you respect the other person's opinion. At the next networking event, seek out that person just to say hello and express appreciation for making a connection.

Never Sell At Networking Events: We have all been to parties or events where one person is always talking about himself/herself, bragging and in general being self centred, seeking only to achieve his/her objectives with little regard for anyone else. Don't be that person. You shouldn't sell at networking events, you are there simply to increase your brand awareness, make connections and be a good connector for helping others make connections. Your selling activity should take place elsewhere.

Online Networking and Connections: People will definitely check you out online to find out more about you. So make sure your profile is up to date and accurately reflects what you do and you're (USP). Use online platforms to connect with others. Seek out the people you are connected to that might be able to introduce you to the people you want to meet. Often organisations focus only on their organisation; what they produce or provide and not what the end customer receives. Looking at a supply chain network enables firms to look at the overall movement of materials and information from start to end, allowing organisations to see the value in creating partnerships and the value in working together to ensure the best possible value is provided to the end customer. Supply chains and supply networks both describe the flow and movement of materials and information, by linking organisations together to serve the end customer. The network describes a more complex structure, where organisations can be cross-linked and there are two-way exchanges between them.

Material Handling and Warehousing:

Material handling is the movement, protection, storage and control of materials and products throughout manufacturing, storing, distribution, consumption and disposal stages. As a process, material handling incorporates a wide range of manual, semi-automated and automated equipment and systems that support logistics and make the supply chain work. Their application helps with:

- Forecasting
- Resource allocation
- Production planning
- Flow and process management
- Inventory management and control
- Customer delivery
- After-sales support and service

A company's material handling system and processes are put in place to improve customer service, reduce inventory, shorten delivery time, and lower overall handling costs in manufacturing, distribution and transportation.

Market Research:

Market research is a technique used both by prospective entrepreneurs and established businesses to gather and analyse information about the market their business operates in. Market research is used for developing effective strategies, weighing the pros and cons of a proposed decision and determining the future path of the business. Keep your business' competitive edge sharp with keen market research skills! Have a goal for your research in mind. Market research should be designed to help you and your business become more competitive and profitable. If your market research efforts don't eventually give your company some benefit, it would be time wasted and time that could have been better spent doing something else. Before you begin, it's important to define exactly what you want to figure out through your market research. Your research may lead you in unexpected directions, this is perfectly fine. However, it's not a good idea to start your market research without at least having one or more concrete goals in mind.

Below are just a few of the types of questions you may want to consider when designing your market research:

- Is there a need in that market that my business/company can fill? Researching priorities and spending habits of your customers can help you determine whether it's a good idea to attempt to do business in a certain market in the first place.

- Are my products and services meeting needs of my customers? Researching your customers' satisfaction with your business can help you increase your business's competitiveness.

- Am I pricing my products and services effectively? Researching your competition's practices and wide-scale market trends can help ensure you're making as much money as possible without hurting your business.

Develop a plan for gathering information efficiently. Just as it's important to know what you want your research to accomplish ahead of time, it's also important to have an idea of how you can realistically reach this goal. Again, plans can and do change as research progresses. However, setting a goal without having any idea of how to achieve it is never a good idea for market research.

Below are questions to consider when drafting a market research plan:

Will I need to find extensive market data? Analysing existing data can help you make decisions about the future of your business, but finding useful, accurate data can be difficult.

Will I need to do independent research? Creating your own data from surveys, focus groups, interviews, and more can tell you a lot about your company and the market it operates in, but these projects require time and resources that can also be spent on other things.

Be prepared to present your findings and to decide on a course of action. The purpose of market research is to make an impact on actual decisions that you take about your business/company. When you do market research, unless your business is a sole proprietorship, usually, you'll need to share your findings with other people in the company and have a plan of action in mind. If you have superiors, they may or may not agree with your plan of action, but few will disagree with trends displayed by your data unless you've made errors in the way you gathered your data or conducted your research.

Distribution Channels:

A distribution channel is the path by which all goods and services must traverse to reach the intended consumer. Conversely, it also describes the pathway payments make from the end consumer to the original vendor.

Distribution channels can be short or long and depend on the number of intermediaries required to deliver a product or service.

However, goods and services sometimes pass to consumers through multiple channels; a combination of short and long will do well for your business. While increasing the number of ways a consumer can find a good can increase sales, it can also create a complex system that sometimes makes distribution management difficult. In addition, the longer the distribution channel, the less profit a manufacturer might get from a sale because each intermediary charges for its service.

While a distribution channel can sometimes seem endless, there are 3 main types of channels, all of which include a combination of a producer, wholesaler, retailer and end consumer. The first channel is the longest because it includes all 4: producer, wholesaler, retailer and consumer. The FMCG (fast moving consumer goods) manufacturing industries in India are perfect examples. In this industry, products cannot be sold to the consumer directly. It operates in the three-tier system; a manufacturer first sells a product to a wholesaler who in turn sells to a retailer. The retailer then sells the product to the end consumer.

The second channel is the one where the producer sells directly to a retailer who sells the producer's product to the end consumer. This means the second channel contains only one intermediary. The home appliance industry for example, largely sells its products directly to reputable retailers. The third and final channel is a direct-to-consumer model where the producer sells products directly to the end consumer. Flipkart using its own platform to sell Kindles to its customers is an example of a direct model. This is the shortest distribution channel possible.

Improving Customer Loyalty:

Make the Relationship More Than Official or Business Like: As a company, we tend to talk to our customers only when they do business with us or when they are in need of our support. This level of engagement will never make us their favourite. Understanding their likes and dislikes and getting to know them close boosts loyalty. Broaden your relationship with customers and watch how things change for the better.

Create Reliability: When we keep our promises, we show our customers that they are not taken for granted. Also, their respect for us grows with every commitment we meet. Customer loyalty automatically increases when customers remember us for our sincerity, instead of thinking of us for our inability to deliver on our promises.

Always Give: Giving need not always be in the form of rewards or discounts. Delivering products ahead of the schedule is also a great way to enhance customer experience and be remembered for a good reason. Through such acts, customers understand that we are trying our best to out-do ourselves and our customers' expectations.

Be Truthful Even If It Means No Business for You: As our customers have different tastes, not all of our products might interest them. We must accept that and not force anything on them. If you would have the heart to recommend a competitor's product because it meets a customer's requirement better, your customer will never forget that. The very fact that a company is more interested in the customer's needs than its business will go a long way in building customer loyalty.

Technology Is Good, But the Human Touch Is Much More Valuable: Though we are highly dependent on technology for efficiency, there are lots of areas where automated machines cannot answer all of our customers' queries. Having one-to-one interactions with our customers makes it easy for both of us to understand each other better. Customers open up more when there is a human voice with an understanding tone on the other end rather than hearing the beep of a machine.

Be Caring and Expressive: We might find that some of our regular customers haven't paid us a visit in a long time. It is definitely not a good thing. We must immediately express that we miss them and if the situation permits, invite them back with some kind of reward or gift. The customers need to know that their presence makes a huge difference! If we do not care to let them know, they would not care to visit us either. Let us show some love that our customers cannot help but be loyal to us.

Return on Investment (ROI):

Return on Investment is a performance measure, used to evaluate the efficiency of an investment or compare the efficiency of a number of different investments. ROI measures the amount of return on investment, relative to the investment's cost. To calculate ROI, the benefit or return of an investment is divided by the cost of the investment. The result is expressed as a percentage or a ratio. ROI is a popular metric because of its versatility and simplicity. Essentially, ROI can be used as a basic measure of an investment's profitability. The calculation is not complicated, relatively easy to interpret, and has a range of applications.

If an investment's ROI is not positive, or if other opportunities with higher ROIs are available, these signals can help investors eliminate or select the best options.

ROI can be used in conjunction with Rate of Return, which takes into account a project's time frame. One may also use Net Present Value (NPV), which accounts for differences in the value of money over time, due to inflation. The application of NPV when calculating the rate of return is often called the Real Rate of Return. The simple ROI is easy to do, but it is loaded with a pretty big assumption. It assumes that the total month-over-month sales growth is directly attributable to the marketing campaign. For the marketing ROI to have any real meaning, it is vital to have comparisons. Monthly comparisons particularly, the sales from the business line in the months prior to the campaign launching can help show the impact more clearly.

Developing a Sales Strategy:

Jumping into selling your product or service without planning how you will go about it is likely to yield far poorer results than if you adopt a strategic approach to your sales. Use your sales strategy as part of your business plan, to help you convince your bank/funding agency manager or potential investors. Make sure you update and review your sales strategy regularly.

Purpose of a Sales Strategy: A sales strategy sets out, in detail, how you will get your product or service in front of people who need it. Looking at it strategically will give you a comprehensive, methodical approach to ensuring you're marketing your business correctly, and you are approaching the right clients. A sales strategy can be based on your business and marketing plans. It looks at how you will deliver objectives set out in your marketing plan, as well as how you have chosen to segment your target market and how you will fund your marketing activities. A sales strategy is not the same as a marketing strategy. Whereas marketing is about getting your name out there and tempting new customers or rekindling interest in your business, a sales strategy is more about how you close the deal. In order to build a comprehensive strategy for your entire business, you will need to sit down and come up with a different sales strategy for each of your product lines. While they may all end up looking very similar, it's important to be aware of any subtle differences between your products and the customers who pay for them.

Improving Customer Service:

Customer service is the golden key to any successful business – if you don't have it, act fast and make it a priority. Customer service has evolved over the past years; instead of just one-on-one private interaction in person or via phone call, it is now evolved around social media as well. Various social media platforms are available for consumers to connect with their favourite brands almost instantly, making customer service much more crucial than ever before. Want to improve your customer service and increase sales performance? The following will help you gain insight into what to do in order to improve your customer service and increase your sales performance:

Clarify Your Mission and Break the Mission Into Specific Goals: Begin by understanding your business niche. What do you do best? Who needs what you do? How do you best approach these prospects? These are some questions you might want to stop and think about before you start diving in. Once you have figured this part out, it's now time to think about your weekly, monthly, and yearly goals. Start off by setting results goals to measure your progress, and track them closely. Increase your activity and measure the results.

Seek Feedback from Customers: Receiving feedback from your customers is essential in order to improve your business overall. Find out ways to solicit feedback, for instance, as a business request telephone numbers or email addresses to text or email surveys to them. Regardless of the manner, the important thing is identifying whether your business is meeting or exceeding your customer's expectations. Use the comments you receive to increase your sales by improving your products or service.

Respond Quickly: The most significant aspect of social media is that it works fast and is easy to use. It allows brands to quickly connect with their consumers via any of their platforms. Consumers are now also using social media platforms to voice their experiences online and expect to receive a response from their favourite companies within a 24–48 hour gap.

Cross-Sell At Every Turn: A great way to increase sales without the added cost of a separate marketing campaign is to make sure your sales reps are cross selling at every turn. Cross selling is the act of offering new products and services along with those in which the customer may have expressed an initial interest. So for instance, if consumer purchases a smartphone and if the salesperson offers him/her a mobile cover and a tempered glass scratch guard to go along with the purchase, then the salesperson is involved in a cross-selling activity. The more you add on, the more sales you receive. It's crucial to train your sales and customer service agents in this type of skill because it is an effective way to increase sales.

Provide Educational and Appropriate Information: Customer service should not only be about being responsive, but you should also be offering customers with knowledge related to your brand. Sharing knowledge can help to provide value to customers and give them a place to go if they need advice.

Create Referrals Through An Incentive: Customers love incentives – so the perfect way to gain referrals is to have your customers refer your business to their friends and family and in return receive an incentive. A study that analysed a bank referral reward programme showed that new customers who were referred to the bank by existing ones were 18 percent more likely to stay with the bank and generated 16 percent more profits.

Take Time to Train Your Frontline Staff: The heart of your customer service operation should rest with your frontline staff. These employees are the face of your business and if trained well, it gives your business the opportunity to define how your customers perceive your company's products and services. You want to make sure these employees are skilled at conflict resolution, are empowered to exceed your customers' expectations and have the kind of winning personalities that your business patrons are unlikely to forget.

Take the Responsibility But Not the Credit: If you are the team leader of your business; your company looks to you for direction and supports your effort. In order to build a strong support team willing to go the extra mile when you need it, you need to appreciate your team by giving them credit for everything that goes right, and take the blame when it goes wrong.

Go the Extra Mile: As a successful business organisation, going the extra mile for your customers is vital. Going that extra mile can change a stressful or ordinary experience into a positive and remembering one, highlighting the brand's ability to not only empathise with its customers but to also enact real change that positively affects them as well. Showing that you care about your customers allows your customers to appreciate your services and want to continue to build a relationship with you.

Take Advantage of Negative Feedback: It's no secret that nobody likes to hear the negative comments about themselves or their business, but instead of getting hurt take it as a great opportunity to turn your customers' experience around. Nobody runs a perfect business with perfect customers, receiving any kind of feedback helps you and your company to learn and grow as you go. Addressing a complaint or bad experience shows customers that their voices are being heard and that each individual is a valued customer. Increasing engagement and value can increase customer loyalty, resulting in continued engagement and sales.

INTROSPECTION QUESTIONNAIRE

1. What is the difference between marketing & sales?
   _____
   _____

2. Specify the sales know how that you have learnt from this chapter.
   _____
   _____

3. What is a distribution channel and whether it is advantageous over direct sales?
   _____
   _____

4. What is ROI and why is it important in every business?
   _____
   _____

5. Why is feedback from your customers on your product is necessary?
   _____
   _____

Chapter – 5

"Stay focussed on your goals 100%, nothing can stop you"

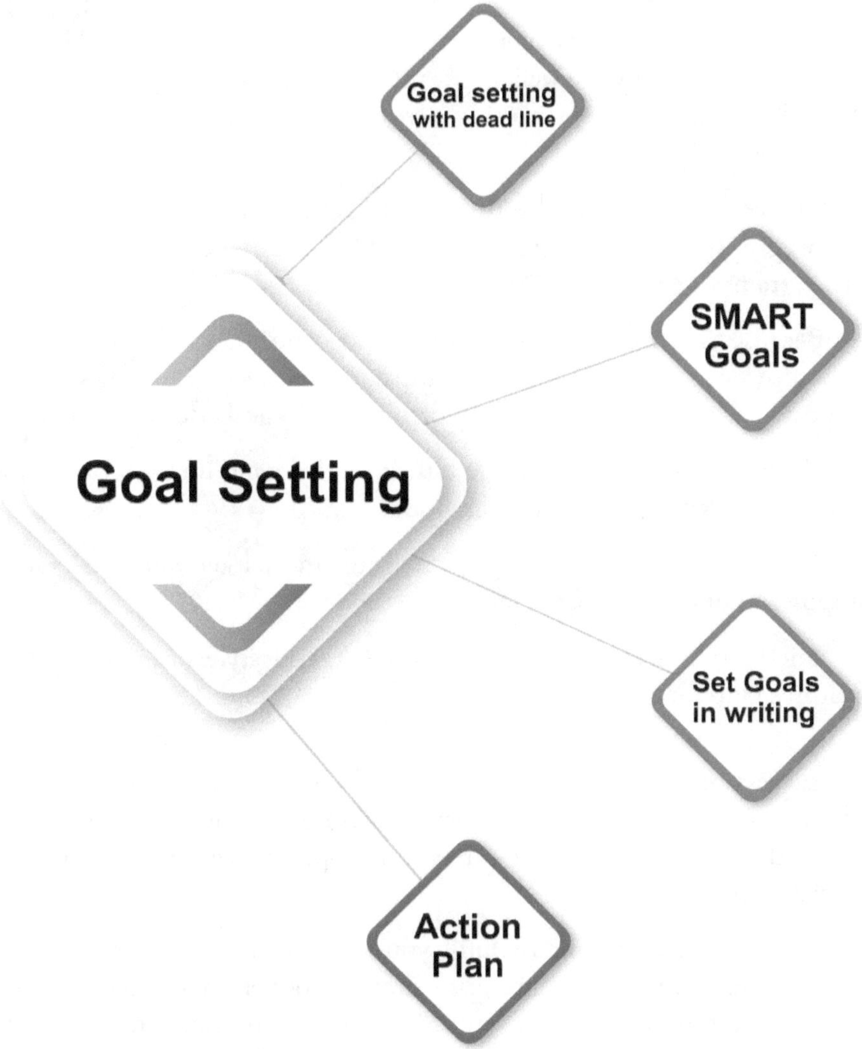

Goal Setting

- Goal setting with dead line
- SMART Goals
- Set Goals in writing
- Action Plan

Purnima Goyal – Silverine:

There is an increasing demand for physical, emotional and spiritual well-being among city dwellers.

Silverine Spa & Salon is a unisex wellness brand launched in Jaipur by well known beautician Purnima Goyal with a view to providing physical wellness through which one can aspire to achieve emotional and spiritual well-being.

Shishor Goyal, her partner and husband joined forces with her, and aligned his family silver jewellery business adding a new dimension to the spa and salon entity by promoting silver jewellery in line with the theme of physical wellness.

The couple launched Silverine in 2015 as a franchise with Cleopatra, the biggest spa and salon in Jaipur in terms of its sheer physical size. Cleopatra has 13 centres in Punjab.

Because Silverine was based on the second floor of a mall, they embarked on a unique marketing campaign to attract customers to climb 2 floors ensuring that it would be worth their physical effort.

Silverine reached out to more customers by tying up with banks and retailers to offer spa facilities at discounts.

Their next aim is to target the tourism market and Mr. Goyal proposes to offer hotel guests affordable services.

The couple is also proposing to launch a lifestyle magazine and an exclusive club for salon memberships.

"The success of any business or venture will depend on setting short-term, mid-term and long-term goals with achievable deadlines irrespective of whether the business or venture caters to non-public, enterprise, own family or social segments of society."

In case you really want to fulfil your dream of owning an enterprise, it's critical to define your enterprise dreams sooner than later. For some people, the aim of launching a venture may be the freedom that they get to do what they want to do when they want to do without others telling them otherwise. For a few, the aim of launching an enterprise maybe an economic cushion.

Setting goals is an integral a part of selecting a business that truly suits your personality and character. In the end, if your enterprise does not meet your dreams, you probably may not be happy waking up every morning and trying to make the business or venture a success. Ultimately you may end up not making the earnest attempt to make your concept work. So setting up a successful business may not be just dreaming what you want to do, but to work out tangible plans in the short-term, mid-term and long-term so that you significantly increase possibilities of achieving your dream at the very outset. Business dreams can be like a painting in a framework and the painting will have to fit the right framework to be attractive. Similarly, a business dream has to be set in a set time frame to be successful. The following can help set the right goals for the success of your business:

1. Set Goals that Motivate You:

When you set goals for yourself:

- Make sure it is motivating and value added.
- Motivation is the key to achieving goals.
- Set goals of high priorities in your life.
- Goal achievement requires commitment.
- Should have "I must do this" attitude to make your Goal a reality.

2. Set SMART Goals:

Specific

      Measurable

           Attainable

                  Relevant

                        Time Bound.

Set Specific Goals:

- Goal must be clear and well defined.
- Analyse "Where you are now"
- Fix your goal precisely "Where you want to go"

Set Measurable Goals:

- Fix amounts and dates in your goals for Success.
- Generic goal: "Want to Score High Marks"
  – There is No time limit and No Measure for success.
- Specific measure: This Semester & 90%.

Set Attainable Goals:

- Make sure that your Goals are achievable.
- Always set Realistic and Challenging goals
- Unachievable Goals:
  – will only demoralize yourself and erode your confidence.

Set Relevant Goals:

- Goals: Should be relevant to the direction in your life and career.
- Develop the focus you need to get ahead and do what you want.

Set Time-Bound Goals:

- Goals must have a deadline.
- Make your efforts based on the deadline.
- Achieve your Goals well within specified time.
- Enjoy your success.
- The Three Time frames:

    a. The Short-term Goal should be achievable in a duration of a few weeks to a maximum of 1 year.

    b. The Mid-term Goal should be achievable within 1 to 3 years.

    c. The Long-term Goal can be achievable in 5, 10 or a maximum of 2 years. At the outset, set practical Goals.

3. Set Goals in Writing:

- Writing down a goal makes it real and tangible.
- Use the word "will" instead of "would like to" or "might."
- Frame your goal statement positively.
- Make a To-Do List that has your goals at the top.
- Write your Action Program.
- Post your goals visible – on your walls, desk, computer monitor.

Key Points of Goal Setting:

- Clearly define exactly what you want.
- Understand why you want it the first place.
- Set your goals with confidence and enjoy the outcome.

ACTION PLAN

Make an Action Plan:

- Action Plan is the main step in the process of goal setting.
- Write down all the steps needed for your Action Plan.
- Cross each step off as and when you complete it.
- Make progress towards your ultimate goal.
- Build in reminders to keep yourself on track.
- Review/Evaluate your goals periodically.
- Change action plan if it is absolutely necessary.
- Make sure the relevance, value, and necessity remain high.

INTROSPECTION QUESTIONNAIRE

1. How will you set a goal for a successful business?

_____

_____

2. Why should there be a deadline for every goal?

3. Why should we prepare an Action Plan?

4. Why should the Goals to be reviewed periodically?

Chapter – 6

*"If you are not planning for your success,
You are planning for your failure"*

Planning

1 Perfectly written Business Plan

2 Marketing Strategy

3 Accomplishing Plan effectively

> ### Kailash Katkar – Quick Heal Technologies:
>
> The story of Kailash Katkar is a typical rags to riches story as he began his professional career at a calculator and radio repair shop. In 1990, he ventured on to start his own repair business for calculators.
>
> In 1993, his brother developed a new antivirus model for solving computer maintenance issues. Despite having no formal education, the Katkar brothers took Quick Heal Technologies to dizzy heights.

Proper planning helps a company chart the right direction for fulfilling of its dreams. The process starts with reviewing the current operations of the organisation and figuring out what needs to become operational in the next 12 months. From there on further planning includes envisioning the results the business/venture wants to gain, and determining steps that are vital to reach the defined destination or achievement, whether it is measured in monetary terms, or goals that include being the highest-rated business among customers.

In corporations, making plans is a control process involved with defining goals for the business enterprise's future path and figuring out on missions and resources to reach set goals. To reach goals, managers may also combine plans together with a business plan or an advertising plan. Planning usually has a motive such as achieving a positive set of goals.

Main Characteristics of Making Plans in Businesses Are:

Planning will increase the overall performance level of a corporation. It safeguards against pitfalls involved in present day business activities. It utilises with maximum efficiency available time and resources.

The 4 questions based on which a corporation chalks out a plan are: Where are we today in terms of our business or planning method? Where are we headed? In which direction can we need to head? How are we going to get there?

A good plan is a written document of your business' future, a document that clearly tells what you plan to do and how you plan to do it. The seeds for a good plan can be some random thoughts that you have jotted down on the back of an envelope. That can be systematically developed into a good plan. Business plans are inherently strategic. You begin with sure assets and skills with a view to getting to the set goal usually within 3 to 5 years by which time your business will have a one set of defined sources and skills as well as profitability with some fixed asset base. Your plan basically indicates how you propose to reach that set goal in that time frame.

7 Steps to a Perfectly Written Business Plan Earlier Than Writing Your Plan:

- How lengthy your plan ought to be?
- When must you write it?
- Who needs a marketing strategy?
- Why must you write A business plan?
- Decide your goals and targets.
- Define your financing needs.
- Decide how you will implement your plan.
- Make sure to add marketing elements.

The Elements of Your Business Plan:

- A marketing strategy.
- How to start a commercial enterprise.
- Updating the plan.
- Enhancing the marketing strategy.
- Business plan equipment.
- Business plan software.
- Books and the way-to manuals.
- Business plan templates.
- Samples of other business plans.

What Must a Marketing Strategy Consist of?

There aren't many guidelines, but some of the elements to include are:

- Business profile.
- Market studies.
- Operational approach.
- Merchandise and/or services.
- Advertising plan.
- Financial method.

Earlier the better to start working on the plan. You also need to keep in mind the subsequent key questions to assist you in writing the marketing strategy once you are geared for the endeavour.

- Have you thoroughly debated your business idea so that you have a good know how of ways your business will perform?
- Have you researched your enterprise idea to decide if there is a want for it the market?
- Have you completed the feasibility study to assess the anticipated level of success?
- Have you got the funds required to start and develop the Enterprise?
- Are you organised to make investments large time into the enterprise to get it up and sustain on the long-term?

HOW FREQUENTLY SHOULD I REVIEW MY BUSINESS PLAN?

Evolving and evaluating plans is an ongoing process for a successful business or commercial activity. Plans need to be updated according to changing circumstances of the business environment.

Methods to Be Followed for Accomplishing the Plan Effectively:

You Need to Be Determined About Your Business Choice with a Firm Resolve: The first step in achieving your goal is to make sure that you are determined what you want to do without a wavering mind. Thinking positive and focussing can help achieve goal on hand, so work with a determined motive of what you set out to achieve.

Visualise Yourself Achieving Your Goal: Always keep the image of what you want to achieve in front of your mind is an oft quoted statement of elders. Having determined your goal of business, work towards achieving it keeping the big picture in mind. You can achieve success by changing your mind to suit your needs of achieving business success.

Draw a Practical Plan: Draw a plan for the course you need to take to accomplish your business goal. Create action steps to follow by discovering the essential route. Choosing the right path is crucial for you to achieve your goal and accomplishments.

Write Down Your Goals: It is not just enough if you have an idea or thought in mind, you need to jot it down and expand it to become a fruitful plan. Writing down your thoughts, expanding them into plans and writing down steps you will take to achieve your goals will turn out to be your stepping stones to success.

Check Your Development Plan: While exuding optimism in executing your plans, you need to have a pessimistic outlook when checking and detailing your plans. You need to constantly look at your hourly planner, daily planner, weekly planner, monthly planner and yearly planner to make sure everything is going on schedule. Keep a hawk eye on all elements of your plan, monitor the situation closely to make sure you are making progress as chalked out in our plan and charted out in action.

You may have to take corrective measures due to ongoing situations or market sentiments. Make sure you have a tab on all that is happening your business environment with a single-minded devotion to achieving your business goal. You have to alert and keeping a watchful eye on every aspect of your business venture from setting up, installing machinery if needed, procuring raw materials to dispatching the end product to the intended consumer/customer to ensure that there is no distraction or deviation in your plans in achieving your business goal.

INTROSPECTION QUESTIONNAIRE

1. "If you fail to plan, you are planning to fail" – Define.

   _____

   _____

2. How would you plan a business before starting?

3. Explain whether periodical Review of business plan is necessary.

4. What is marketing strategy?

5. In case of introducing a new product, what would be your marketing strategy?

Chapter – 7

*"Mission without a Vision is merely a dream;
Mission with a Vision can change the world"*

Product • People • Process

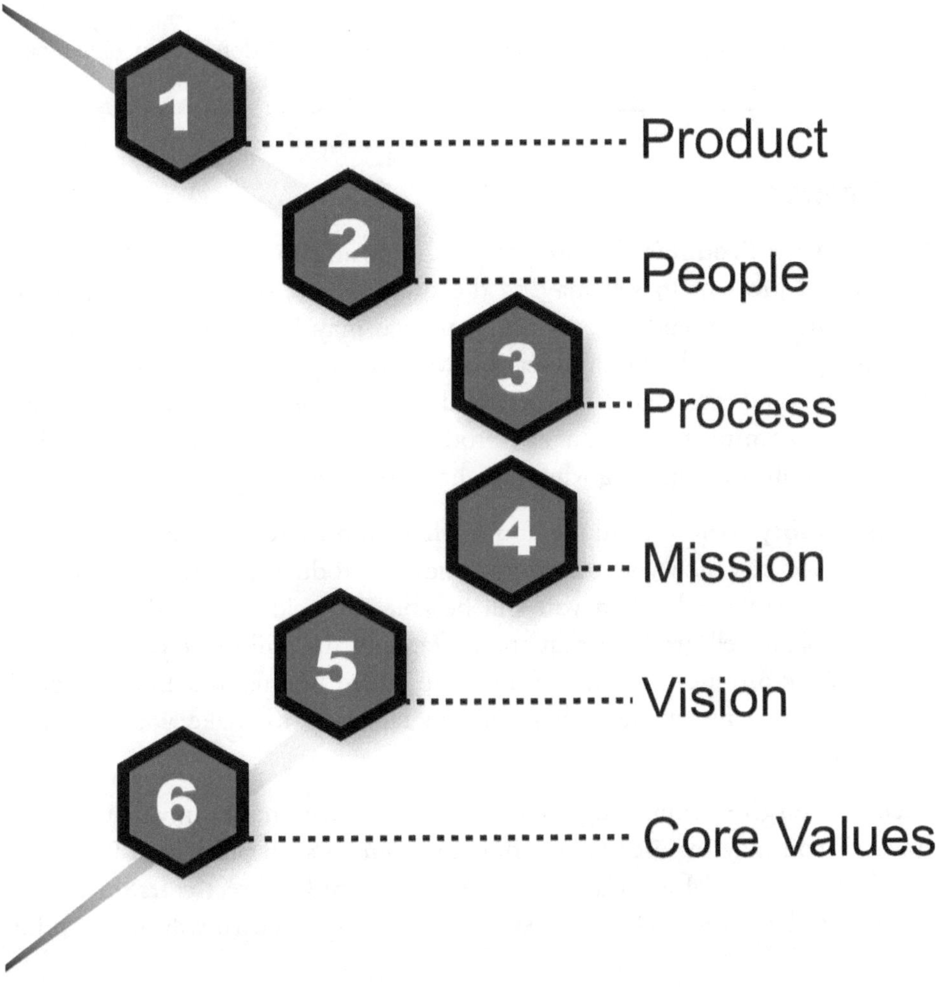

1. .... Product
2. .... People
3. .... Process
4. .... Mission
5. .... Vision
6. .... Core Values

> ### *Patricia Narayan:*
>
> Patricia Narayan is a symbol of perseverance as 30 years ago she started selling food from a mobile cart on a beach. All odds were against her as she was battling a failed marriage and providing for her children.
>
> Today she owns a chain of restaurants with her growth transcending from 2 people working for her to 2 hundred people working in her restaurants. Lifestyle changes also happened with her revenue steadily increasing from 50 paise per day to Rs. 2 lakh per day.
>
> As a culmination of over 30 years of hard work, she was bestowed with the FIICI Entrepreneur of the Year Award. Her ambition is to build a brand.
>
> She advices entrepreneurs never to lose self confidence and never to compromise on quality.

1. PRODUCT

Choose Your Products: In case you are proposing to start a retail business, choosing a product to sell may be the toughest decision you will need to make. Choices are endless and the challenge may be overwhelming at the beginning. Essentially the product you want to target in retail business must have a demand and make it worthwhile your effort in investing in it. So before you commit to a product or product line, keep in mind the following elements while determining what merchandise to sell.

Marketability: Before thinking about what product to promote, decide the marketplace in which you want to promote a product. As soon as your sort out your client needs, then you will be able to decide on product base. If you are able to sell products that are in demand that will make your business viable. Your product may not attract the entire population, but it should cater to the niche segment that you are targeting to make your business successful.

Income Margin: Selling huge price tag items is commonly more profitable, however you may require greater effort to promote such products. While you consider the price of a product, calculate direct and indirect costs, including overheads. This is to make sure that the profit that you earn will make up for all your expenses and still leave a fairly good margin for you. Suppose you sell 50 pieces of a product X for Rs. 100 with a profit margin of Rs. 30 (the actual cost of the product being Rs. 70), you must ensure that profit gained by selling 50 items is feasible and worthwhile. You have to decide the final balance of competitively pricing your product and earning a suitable profit.

Consumable: Pick a product that fetches a regular income such as a consumable item that is in continuous demand in more than one retailer. By choosing a product that consumers will repeatedly buy, you can build a rapport with them and use that for promoting other products. And if a customer visits your outlet repeatedly for buying a recurring product there are greater chances of him picking other products also, so that your business venture is sustained.

What's Popular: When it comes to promoting merchandise based on popularity, timing is extraordinarily important. New businesses and products may be a tremendous boost in your commercial enterprise but you will want to be at the start of the product lifecycle so that you can be successful. Learning to pick a warm product before it becomes hot is a treasured ability that comes from knowing your marketplace.

Competition: Competition is healthy and there are approaches other than quantity and price on which a smaller store can compete with large retailers. Alternatively, the greater particular the product, the much less danger of competition. For this reason choose a unique product which has demand in the marketplace.

Private Label: One manner to guarantee having a definitely precise product line is to make the object yourself. Another way is to partner with a small business establishment that makes a product you would enjoy promoting. Additionally, consider private label merchandise (products which are generally manufactured or provided by one company, then labelled with another company's brand) so as to boost your product's brand image.

Focus On Quality: When identifying which product to sell in your shop ask yourself, "Is this a product I would give my dearest friend? "The answer to your question will decide what products you want to sell as a retailer.

Range: Keep your product supply range simple and in need with market demands, this will make your advertising pitch as well as sales strategy easy. As far as you have products compatible with market demands, your business will continue to thrive. Some useful tips before choosing products for sale:

- Will you buy it and use it yourself?
- Are you able to see yourself getting excited about this product or service?
- Might you promote it to a person you know personally well?
- Is there an actual want for the product in the current market situation?
- Will you consider yourself promoting this product in a sustained manner?

The key to having a successful business enterprise is to understand your merchandise and to trust products that you are selling. If you do not accept as true the product you are selling then you probably might not be successful at selling it. Brainstorm with friends, family or staff who understand your mindset and you will find a product or product line that meets your goals of a successful retail business.

2. PEOPLE

To achieve success in any business, you need to recognise and value human beings. Some business leaders think that business is all about technology, money, production approaches, or delivery chain. But it is not true, all successful businesses revolve around human needs.

Without people, every product in the world would be worthless. Human beings are the final consumers of each product. Even in business-to-business opportunities, people make selections about what to buy and when.

Business leaders tend to focus on building and sustaining competitive advantage. Businesses try to compete on price, quality or design, which only provide temporary advantages. The only lasting competitive gain is information your organisation possesses – and that your competition may lack – about the people your business serves.

Such information enables your firm to make loyalty extra handy than disloyalty. It will become easier for customers also to deal with you. Information about your customers and regularly meeting their demands make for fair and sustainable profit as you don't have to spend money on promotional activities that your customers don't bother about. Some managers despise the idea that people matter. They assume business success is all about handling the numbers; this is why you notice companies slicing employees to boost income. But this is a very, very short-term strategy. By cutting employees an organisation loses that much amount of information learnt about customers and in turn affecting the relationship that has been built about your business. So taking people out of a business can hurt businesses in the long-term.

Irrespective of technology or the expertise of the higher management, including CEOs, it is imperative for a business to invest in the right people to ensure success.

3. PROCESS

Business Process Management (BPM) is an integrated system to be aware of, design, execute, report, reveal and manipulate both automated and non-automatic business processes to obtain steady, focussed results aligned with a company's strategic goals. BPM entails planned, collaborative and increasingly era-aided definition, development, innovation, and management of end-to-end commercial enterprise procedures that permit an organisation to satisfy its enterprise objectives with greater agility.

BPM permits an organisation to align its enterprise tactics to its business approach as well as maintain an effective performance approach with precise coordination within a department, within an organisation or between agencies involved in the business activities of an organisation.

4. ADVERTISING AND MARKETING STRATEGIES

Advertising and marketing campaigns both traditional and non-traditional methods today play a huge role in the success of any business or new venture. Depending on how much of funds you can allocate for promoting your product, you can choose one of the following or all the methods to ensure a better brand reach for your products.

Think Out of the Box: Social media has today become a useful tool for business to promote their products, including brick and mortar agencies. The first step will be to create an informative website and then promote using other social media platforms such as Facebook or Twitter. The website presence can be further boosted through search engine submissions. But make your posts interesting and effective for prospective consumers.

Branding: Is a very important promotional tool, which is based on how you understand the needs of your customers and how you propose to fulfil their demands. A well branded product will have a great impact on the consumer for which it is important to choose a relevant and good logo. Once etched strongly in the minds and hearts of your consumers, your brand logo will become a symbol of assurance. Consumers will then spread your brand awareness through word of mouth, which is a good indirect marketing and advertising resource. So building a strong brand with an ideal logo will help sustain your business and ensure success in the long-term.

5. VISION, MISSION, AND CORE VALUES

Vision: A vision statement clearly explains your business goals and how you propose to achieve them. The vision statement needs to be percolated down to all staff members of your business organisation. While being creative and imaginative make sure that your business goals are practically achievable with set time frames and written in precise language. Think your vision, discuss it and then jot it down committing sufficient time for it can be the roadmap for the success of your proposed business venture.

Mission: A vision statement needs to be backed by a good mission statement, which actually outlines how you proposed to achieve your objectives of becoming a good businessman and achieve your set business goals. The mission statement can address the following:

- What are the opportunities or goals that the business enterprise proposes to address?
- Having decided the business opportunity, how does the business/organisation propose to address the opportunity?
- What are the sources – funding, human resources, raw materials and other resources – that will be tapped to meet the business requirements?
- What concepts or ideals will guide the enterprise or business in taking forward its professional activities?

Core Values: While explaining the above organisation can also in simple terms explain its core values based on the following:

1. What the business/organisation will do for its customers?
2. What the business/organisation will do for its employees?
3. What the business/organisation will do for its promoters, owners or proprietors?

This can be brief, but eloquently explain what your organisation/business stands for and how can make a difference for consumers and the society.

INTROSPECTION QUESTIONNAIRE

1. How will you choose a product for your own business?

   _____
   _____

2. What are the elements to be followed while determining a product?

   _____
   _____

3. Why are Employees important for the growth of an organisation?

   _____
   _____

4. How do you define a business process?

   _____
   _____

5. Why branding of your product is necessary and how is it advantageous over non-branded products?

   _____
   _____

6. What is your vision in case of starting a new business?

   _____
   _____

Chapter – 8

"Leadership is always with people not on people"

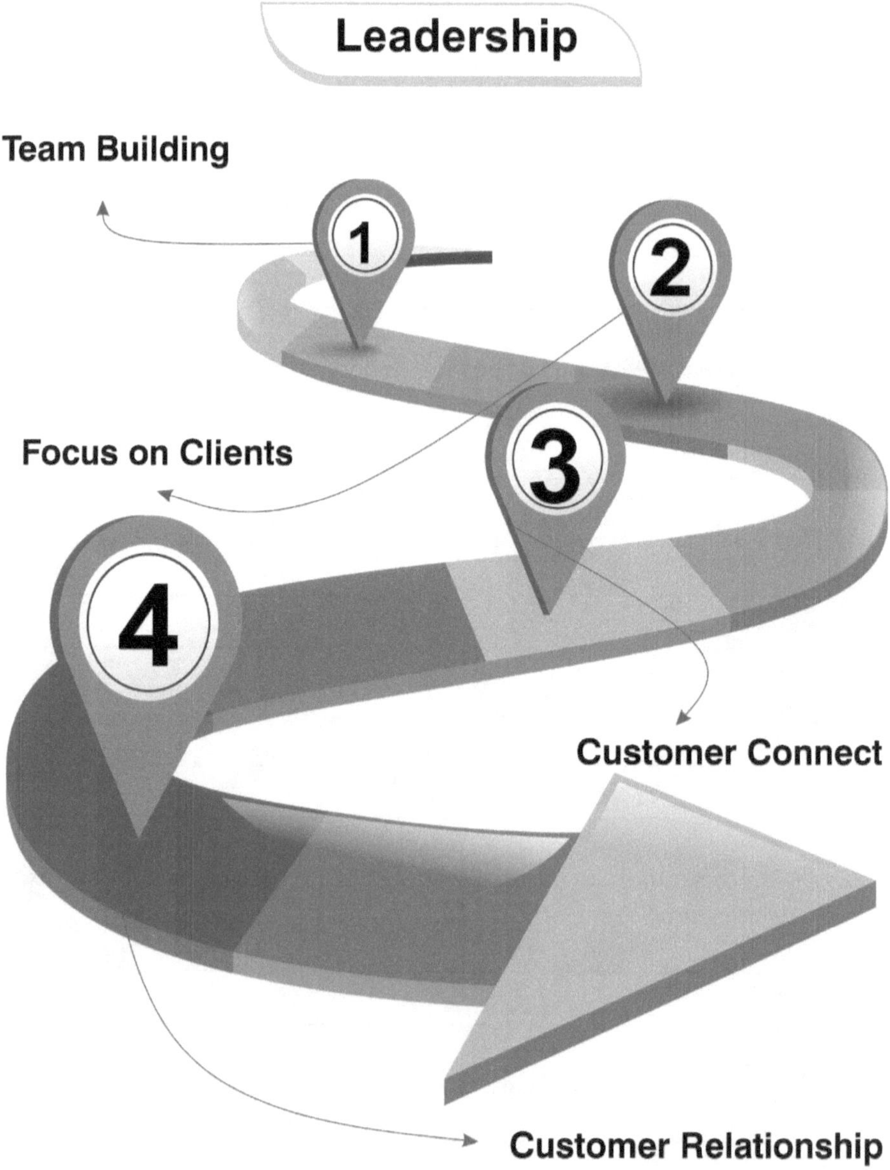

Leadership
Team Building
1
2
Focus on Clients
3
4
Customer Connect
Customer Relationship

> **Dr. Karsanbhai Patel – Nirma:**
>
> In 1969, a new segment was created in the Indian domestic market.
>
> At that time the market for domestic detergents had few companies and it was a yet to be exploited premium segment.
>
> Karsanbhai Patel started making detergent powder in his home in Ahmadabad and started selling the handmade detergent on a door-to-door basis.
>
> He assured his customers a money back guarantee for each pack sold. He offered detergent at a lower cost than the products available in the market then with the aim was of targeting the lower and middle income households.
>
> Thus the success of his brand Nirma can be attributed to marketing a product to suit consumer needs at their doorstep and at the best price. So his sales automatically soared.
>
> From a one man army making Nirma in his backyard in 1969 and selling it door-to-door, the company today employs 14,000 staff members with a total turnover of $500 million!
>
> In 2004, his sales reached a maximum of 800,000 tonnes and Karsanbhai's net worth is expected to reach $1,000 million in no time!

I. TEAM BUILDING: DEVELOPING SECOND LINE LEADERS

Developing Staffing Patterns: Recruiting, training, organising and replacing can be some of the major staffing related issues that a business organisation has to constantly address. Even when you plan to start a business organisation, you need to address these issues. It will be good to clearly assign roles of your staff and also give them the right training to ensure that every staff member fits into your plan of action as perfect cogs in a machine to ensure a smooth pathway to success. It will be your constant endeavour to recognise talent and groom employees so that they feel a part of your success story.

Assign the Function of a Leader To Ensure Systems and Practices are Followed: A team leader does the multi-tasking role of: a) seeing that all sections of an organisation are effectively staffed; b) understands the purpose of the group and how it needs to function; c) is enthusiastic to lead the team in fulfilling its tasks; and d) is skilled and trained well to solve crisis without escalating it to higher levels to ensure a smooth result-oriented performance of the team (the team leader need not always be a charismatic person, but needs to be effective in man management skills; a charismatic team leader can sometimes have a negative impact as some staff members may get frustrated with attention being focussed on just one person).

Human resource is the best capital of any business endeavour and nurturing internal talent can go a long way in the success of an organisation. Building in-house leadership can be one of the biggest assets for any organisation. Especially when an organisation has to face challenges of meeting market changes, expansion or sometimes even top management changes. Under such situations, middle level leaders groomed from within the organisation can play the role of credible influencers within the organisation and to the market forces as well in overcoming any form of crisis. So there is a strong need for any organisation to constantly groom a second level of leadership from within the organisation.

There are any number of case studies as to how some organisations as a cost-cutting measure stopped lateral recruitment of experts and instead focussed on grooming their existing employees to take up responsible roles. The question then arises as to who is responsible to groom the second level. The onus rests on the entire top management of an organisation irrespective of what form it is vis-a-vis proprietary, partnership, private limited or public limited. For example, the CEO, the board of directors and the human resource department can chip in to create the much needed second level of a leadership in an organisation.

II. FOCUS ON CLIENTS

Client Satisfaction: An ideal client of a business organisation can be termed as a consumer who is engaged long-term with the business organisation. Apart from repeat purchase of recurring consumable products or other products, the client or customer will fulfil the following roles:

- Offer valuable feedback on products and organisation.
- Regularly purchases from the business organisation.
- Provides inputs when brand new products are launched.
- Voluntarily promotes the organisation's products to others.

What is your organisation's most precious asset? You may have the best of products, you may have the best of management or shareholders or you may even have the best of staff members, but if you don't have a strong and happy client base your business cannot succeed. Listed are below some of the advantages of having a strong customer base.

Customer Retention Means Improved Sales: Happy clients result in multiplied sales via repeat purchases. Retaining existing customers in a happy frame of mind will be a great asset to any business organisation than trying to woo newer customers.

Great Word of Mouth Promotion: Happy clients are also a great source of indirect marketing as they spread positives about your products and services by word of mouth, which can convert to more business opportunities.

Feedback for Future Development: Happy clients can give valuable feedback and customer interaction about your products and services. The feedback can go a long way in helping you restructure your business processes to meet changing demands and environments.

A few easy approaches to improve your customer service:

Consistency in Client Interaction: Make it easy and simple for clients who seek information about your products or business without having to navigate through different people to access information.

If your business has an online presence, make sure information on the website is also simple and easy to access for customers and focus on building an online relationship maybe even via email.

Take advantage of social listening and respond correctly. Every grievance or situation raised by a consumer through your social media channels is an opportunity to win over clients.

Reach Out: Show your clients that you're continuously placing them first. Make customer support, both offline and online, a dedicated part of your business plan.

Customer Delight: If a customer or client is dissatisfied with your service, don't feel discouraged. This is a great opportunity for you to ramp up your products and services to meet customer satisfaction and delight. Given below are some insights into customer satisfaction and delight:

Always Be Timely:

Timely service is a major key to the success of your business, be it selling a product or providing information. Don't allow your competitors an opportunity to serve your customer faster than you could.

Constantly Focus On Your Customers' Needs:

There is an adage that says, "The Customer is the King." So constantly make sure that you are addressing your customers' needs even listening to them patiently irrespective of whether they appreciate or criticise your products or services. If you have an online presence, make sure that there is an opportunity for customers to comment or remark and also ensure that you promptly reply to their views.

However Give Them What They Need:

Giving customers what they need may be a policy of practicing horses for courses, but on some occasions you should use your discretion on what to give the customer. Convince them and once they realise the advantage of your sales pitch, they will agree to buy what you give.

Attend to Customers' Small Matters Even They Do Not Expect It:

Doing the unexpected such as unscheduled discounts or off season offers will go a long way in winning the hearts of customers. For example, the home appliance industry comes up with big or sometimes even mega offers, including exchanges, during festivals such as Dasara, Diwali or Christmas as well as during New Year.

Give Customers a Point of Contact:

It is crucial to your business to add a human touch when dealing with customers, so give them a specific point of contact (by way of name, maybe designation, phone number and email address), so that customers feel comfortable dealing with human beings rather than the behemoth of an organisation.

Give Clients Their Space:

In today's marketing environment telemarketing and online marketing have become the order of the day, but do not spam your customers' email inbox or keep pounding them with marketing calls, give your customers their space.

Have Guidelines, But Be Flexible:

You may have specific guidelines for dealing with customer issues, but be flexible as each situation in dealing with a customer issue may not be the same.

Inform Your Customers How You Can Assist Them:

Customers generally tend to be independent in choosing products or picking up items from shelves of a store, but sometimes they may not get what they are looking for. Make sure that the "friendly" ground level staff of your organisation are willing to help customers to get what they want.

III. PURCHASER CONNECT & RAPPORT BUILDING

For the success of any business/enterprise, it is crucial for you to develop a rapport with customers and earn their trust especially when making the first contact with customers as the proverb goes, "First impression is the best impression"; this concept must be trickled down to every staff member of your organisation and it can be done by following the simple steps enlisted below:

- Deciding on the proper mindset – be welcoming, enthusiastic, curious and respectful.
- Sending the right signals with your facial expressions and body language.
- Get them to speak and keep talking – be brief, but listen patiently.

How to Establish a Personal Rapport with Customers:

Connecting with your customers should have a personal and human touch, this can help foster a long-term relationship, which indirectly will benefit your business in terms of continued patronage from customers. Listed below are a few means of establishing a rapport:

Model Your Business or Organisation as a Personal Corner Stone: People in general and particularly in India like to talk about some personal issues or what is known as small talk. So as you get familiar with customers regularly visiting your business, it will be great to ask some simple questions like, "How is your mother doing?" or "How is your daughter coping up with college?" Customers will immediately connect to you as a person who cares for their personal well being.

Ask Questions First: Before selling a product find out what your prospective customer is looking for, be polite and gentle as you seek information on your customers' needs. The way you seek information should create confidence in customers that they have come to the right business outlet or organisation.

Woo Your Clients: Sometimes selling can be like wooing and you will have to subtly to convince your customers about your products. It is possible that 3 out of 10 of your customers may be interested in learning more about your products. Over a period of time you can develop such a rapport that you can recall to them that you had emailed an article of relevance based on their product preference.

Make Appropriate Comments: It is essential that you keep the conversation personal without probing too much or discussing too much about their private lives.

Be a Keen Listener: You and staff should also be keen listeners when making a conversation, do not in any way show to your customer that he or she is being ignored or that you are feeling bored by the conversation. Even when there is an attempt to interrupt your conversation by a third person, make sure that your customer gets an appropriate response from you before you divert your attention. Listening to customers is very essential especially for small businesses.

Step Far Away from Your Computer and Telephone: Modern technology may tempt you to use internet or telephone to make conversations even on crucial matters such as meeting a government agency or official who can be a prospective customer or is already a customer and can be a long-term client. But resist those temptations and make time, however busy you are, to make personal calls and have a one-to-one meeting. After decisions are made in such one-to-one meetings, follow-ups can be done via phone or email.

Be Patient: Patience is the ultimate essence of any good business promotion as well as marketing or sales strategy. Inculcate immense patience when dealing with customers and make sure that your staff also deal with customers with patience. Once customers realise that they won't be rushed or hustled they will get a positive impression about your business or organisation.

IV. CLIENT RELATIONSHIP

Money cannot buy one of the most important things you need to promote your enterprise: relationships. How do customer relationships power your commercial enterprise? It is all about locating people who believe in your services or products. And with regards to monitoring those humans down, you have 2 choices:

- You could do all of the legwork yourself and spend huge big on advertising. But that's like rolling a boulder up a hill. You need to power your business into new territory, but each step is difficult and high-priced. There's another less painful – and probably greater profitable-manner:

- You can create an army that will help you push that boulder up the hill instead. How do you try this? You increase relationships with folks who do not just understand your specific knowledge, products or services, but who are also excited and buzzing about what you do. You stay linked with them and deliver them value, and they will touch other people who can benefit your business.

- Powerful relationships don't just occur from one-time meetings at networking events – you don't want a collection of business cards to litter your table. What you want is to ensure the connections that you make continue to grow. Given below are some tips to grow your contacts:

Build Your Network – It Is Your Sales Lifeline: Your community includes business colleagues, professional acquaintances, prospective and existing clients, colleagues, suppliers, contractors and association members, as well as family, friends and your neighbourhood people.

Communication Is a Contact Sport, So Do It Early and Often: Relationships have a short shelf life. Irrespective of how charming, enthusiastic or persuasive you are, nobody will likely remember you from a business card or a one-time meeting. one of the most common mistakes people make is that they arrive home from networking events and fail to follow-up. Make the connections immediately with a follow-up email with a message saying "It was nice to meet you." Send your business information and even if they may not be in need of your business service immediately, they may touch base with you when the need arises.

Utilise All Avenues, Including Online: Email advertising helps build a business relationship at a very affordable or low cost. The email can be in the form of a newsletter highlighting the unique selling proposition of your product or business. If you have developed a good rapport with some of your customers they may help you with indirect marketing by forwarding your emails to their contacts, in what can be called as online word of mouth campaigning.

Praise Loyal Customers and They Will Praise You: Giving small incentives to loyal customers can further strengthen your rapport and improves your chances of a repeat business. Or even just a greeting or a word of praise during the festival season will make you look unique in the eyes of your loyal customers.

Loyal Clients are Your Satisfactory Sales People: So spend the time to build your network with customers and follow-up. Follow-up can be with a simple conversation when they visit your business or it can be in the electronic form. How your nurture your relationship with customers can help you grow your business successfully and help you reach your business goals, especially if you are in the small business segment.

INTROSPECTION QUESTIONNAIRE

1. Why should we develop a second line of leadership?

2. Why customers are important for a business?

3. What is customer delight?

4. How will you develop a strong relationship with your customer?
   _____
   _____

5. How will you convert a passive customer to a prospective customer?
   _____
   _____

Chapter – 9

"Sell the Problem you solve; Not the Product"

Sales

1. Advertising through sports

2. Sales is the key for:
   a) Lifestyles
   b) Self
   c) Business Organization

3. Customer Relationship Management (CRM)

Prem Ganapathy – Prem Sagar Dosa Plaza:

Belonging to an economically backward background, Prem Ganapathy had to do many odd jobs for a meagre monthly income early in his life. He met a person who promised him a better job in Mumbai. To test the genuineness of the person, he asked him for some money and he obliged. Tempted by the offer he left home without informing his parents as a 17-year-old.

He arrived in Mumbai with the stranger who took him to Bandra in a local train and abandoned him there. He overcame his initial jitters and thought of it as an opportunity.

Struggling in a unknown city where he did not know the language, he refused to return home and met a taxi driver who took pity on him. The taxi driver took him to a temple where he was given alms by worshippers. He lived in the temple premises until he found a job in a bakery. He used to wash dishes that were used for making pizzas and slept in the bakery itself. Determined not to return home, 6 months later he found a job as pizza delivery boy and subsequently joined another restaurant as a dish washer.

He faced discrimination and left the hotel to become a tea and coffee supplier to shopkeepers. He earned more than others as a sincere worker. He noted personal tastes of customers on whether they wanted tea to be stronger or sweeter. Seeing his diligence and hard work, another person suggested that he starts a street food stall in joint partnership. In fact the distinct taste and hygiene made his stall an instant hit. But, the person who invested the money however did not share profits with him, instead paid him a meagre salary. That is when Prem Ganapathy decided to start his own food stall.

In 1998, he took a kiosk outside a railway station and started his outlet Prem Sagar Dosa Plaza. The response was good from day one and he soon added variety to his menu. He added a Chinese flavour to his dosas and soon made other varieties such as Paneer Chilli, American Chop Suey, Schezwan and Spring Roll dosas. Within one year of its launch, his Dosa Plaza created 25 varieties of dosas.

In 2003, he opened his outlet in a new mall, and today Dosa Plaza has 35 outlets across India with a an annual turnover of over Rs. 50 million. Rising from a dishwasher to a successful fast food chain entrepreneur, even today he does not hold any contempt for the person who abandoned him at the station and wonders how he is doing. He gets enquiries from Europe and the US for his Dosa Plaza Franchising.

I. USING SPORTS EVENTS TO ADVERTISE YOUR PRODUCT OR BUSINESS

Sales promotion activities can avail various opportunities such as advertising your product, merchandise or business at sports events, which may include sponsoring sports events or branding during sports events. Sales promotion utilising sports activities will include advertising and marketing through window displays, product and promotional material show as well as promotional programmes together with top rate awards and contests.

Important issues that are addressed during such promotion planning are:

1. Status quo of targets
2. Choice of promotional equipment
3. Planning income-merchandising programme
4. Pre-testing
5. Implementation
6. Assessment

Status Quo of Objectives: Sales-advertising targets range according to the target market. If the goal is the purchaser, then it may consist of improved utilisation or building of trial among non-customers or other product users. For intermediaries, objectives may be to encourage off season sales or offsetting competitive promotions. Sales-advertising activities could also be aimed at internal employees as an incentive for their good work.

Choice of Promotional Gear: Promotional targets shape the basis for choosing the most appropriate income-promotion gear. The cost and effectiveness of each object should be assessed with regards to reaching set goals in the target market.

Planning the Income-Promotion Programme: Important choices that need to be made while designing the sales-merchandising programme relate to the timing of the promotion. Also important are the dimensions of incentive, regulations for eligibility, direction and the overall finances for merchandising promotion.

Pre-Checking: This exercise needs to be undertaken in a high-risk market. Checking out in selected market segments can spotlight problems of ambiguity, response charges and provide an indication of price effectiveness.

Implementation: Implementation plans have to encompass 2 important time elements First, it ought to suggest the 'lead time' – the time important to conduct the programme as much as the point where incentives are made available to the general public. Second, the 'sell in time' that is the time period from the date of release to when about 90 to 95 per cent of incentives reach prospective clients.

Evaluation: The performance of the merchandising needs to be assessed against targets set. If targets are precise and quantifiable, then the exercise might seem to be easy. But extraneous factors should also be taken into account for arriving at best results.

II. SALES IS THE KEY FOR

    A. Lifestyles

    B. Self

    C. Business organisation

A) Lifestyles:

Keys to Achievement:

Successful Salespersons/Businessmen Do What They Like to Do: Salespersons doing extraordinarily well generally love their sales career. You need to understand your sales landscape to turn into a profitable painting venture. Focus on right investments, including the investment of time and make sacrifices if needed to ensure that you have the right sales pitch.

Determine Exactly What You Want: Be clear in your sales promotion goals in whatever form even utilising sports events. Studies have shown that people who have written down goals are more likely to reap rich harvests in their sales careers.

Hard Work, Will Power and Perseverance: Like in any profession hard work, determination, dedication and perseverance are the keys to success in the sales field. Having decided to become a businessman throw your heart and soul into your profession at every turn of event to reap success.

Learning Is a Lifelong Experience: Every day is a new day, every opportunity is a new opportunity. Keep yourself abreast of the latest information on your business or products. Every meeting with customers is also a learning experience, I would like to emphasise that there is no end to learning. The more you focus on learning and involving in newer programmes related to your business, the better your returns will be in the long run.

Successful Salespeople Use Their Time Creatively: Creativity is another key to success as your start every day afresh. Before you start your business day give a brief thought to the experience of your previous day and lessons learnt. If you have many tasks for the day jot down by prioritising what you need to do in a chronological order. Make sure you check your notes to make sure you stay on track and success will surely follow you.

Learn from Leaders: Successful people learn from others especially industry leaders. The same is applicable to successful business or sales people. By observing successful leaders one can learn valuable lessons and implement it accordingly in one's business or sales activity.

Focus On Credibility: Credibility and integrity are the most sacred elements of any successful business organisation. Make sure that your business organisation as well as all staff members ensure the highest credibility of your organisation.

Use Inborn Creativity: Every individual is a genius in her or his own way, so tap your creative energy to grow your business or profession. Even when promoting your product or business during a sports event make sure you are at your creative best.

Practice the golden rule "Do unto others as you will have them do unto you": Consider yourself as your consumer and reflect on how you want to be treated? Obviously you would want salespersons to be honest with you. You would want the salesperson to devote time to understand your needs and assist you in meeting your needs. So when you meet a customer treat them in the same way as you imagined you wanted to be treated by a salesperson or a business organisation.

The key to success can also be doing small little things that other people don't do such as don't waste time, keep going and maintain a steady pace.

B) Self:

Define Yourself: First of all define yourself briefly in half-a-minute and this has to be done in a simple way for the customer to understand you quickly. To quote an example:

"I'm from Race Pharmaceuticals, working as Regional Manager for the past 5 years promoting pharmaceutical products in various specialties in Tamil Nadu Region." Now you know who you are, does everyone else know and agree that this is your identity? One of the biggest challenges for those who are selling-themselves is an inability to separate who they truly are from who they are as a product. So, think of "you" as a superman version of yourself. Make a list of your best qualities. Dress the best way that you would dress. Talk the best way that you would talk. In short to be a successful businessman, be the "Best You."

What is the difference between branding, marketing and sales? All too often, we talk about marketing our business when what we really are doing is selling, or talk about working on our branding but what we really are doing is marketing.

- **Selling**: For instance say you are talking to a potential customer about yourself in your 30 seconds early in the morning, You are actually selling your identity.
- **Marketing**: Say you are able to communicate indirectly with a large number of your target customers about your identity through a mailing list or some other marketing channel, then you are marketing your identity to your target audience.

Communicate with Perseverance: In this competitive world, you need to communicate with perseverance and engage with people until you achieve your goal. There was a job opening in a top MNC in Chennai, when I heard about the job opening from the HR Department, I suggested a candidate who I thought was the most deserving for that job. The reason was she was persistently annoying me for a job, reaching out to me via emails and trying her best to hard sell her professional capabilities. She was young, smart and perseverant; hence she got the job in that MNC based on my recommendation.

Be Dynamic: People try to sell themselves, their products or their services to the customers all the time through traditional methods, including sending dull or boring emails. Traditional methods have become outdated and you have to be dynamic in your selling campaign. For example, when the Internet first came to existence it was Internet promotions through advertising emailers or newsletters. But today the Internet has graduated to the Digital Platform, where there are many avenues to tap. So just sending routine emailers won't work, you will have to dynamically change your campaigns to use the broader Digital Marketing platforms to reach out to tech-savvy customers.

C) Business Organisation:

In any organisation, the sales branch performs a pivotal function for the success of the organisation. The ultimate goal of making both ends meet – income versus expenditure – and achieving success through profit can be met by the crucial role played by a sales force in any business.

Convert Leads Into Income: Salespersons are the crucial bridge between a consumer and a product. They will have to make sure that prospective customers can become target consumers with their sales pitch. They can use tools of advertising or marketing to convince customers and close the deal to generate income for the business or organisation.

Take for example, automobile sales wherein a customer first visits a showroom to get firsthand knowledge of products in hand though the customer would have some thoughts or ideas on what he wants to buy. The salesperson as the first point of contact probes the customer to get more information on what the customer is looking for, what are her or his needs, what are her or his capacities, the size of family and need for buying a four-wheeler or two-wheeler.

The salesperson then makes the pitch by suggesting various options and explaining through information brochures to try and meet customer demands. The salesperson will have made the perfect pitch if she or he manages to convince the customer to buy one of the products building on credible information provided during the sales pitch.

Business Success: Financial aspects play a key function in the defining loyalty between a purchaser and a business organisation. Trust and loyalty are the main motives on why a customer would recommend your business organisation to a friend, another member of a family, or write a positive review. So if a customer feels that he is getting a fair deal for his investment then surely he will be your friend in recommending your brand or product to his friends and family. In today's virtual world, online media can be used to target prospective customers and convince them they would be making the best buy – value for money – by investing in your product.

Purchaser Retention: Retaining a customer is another key to the success of a business and this can be done through personal interactions to touch the humane aspect of your prospective client. Instead of cold-shouldered information sharing or explanation, a friendly disposition and personal interaction will help retain a purchaser in any business organisation. And very significantly, following-up on after-sales promises such as quarterly checkups or in the example of the auto industry, doing a thorough after sales service, will ensure customer retention. Attending expeditiously to customer grievances will also help to retain a client with your portfolio. A dissatisfied customer has many options in the market today and will not hesitate to shift loyalty in a jiffy and can cause further damage to your business by painting a negative picture, so make sure all customer grievances – big or small are attended to immediately.

In conclusion, the strength of the sales team goes beyond the financial gains of a business organisation. It can help build a long-term relationship as well as enhance the reputation of your brand.

III. CONSUMER RELATIONSHIP MANAGEMENT (CRM)

Consumer Relationship Management (CRM) helps a business or organisation interact with existing and prospective customers. CRM uses customer and business history to reach out to existing customers to build a positive relationship or attract new customers into the business fold. CRM data is typically compiled with information from various sources of communication both formal and informal, including online platforms, telemarketing and one-to-one interactions, CRM also helps businesses better understand their customers and reorient their business to meet customer demands.

CRM banks on the concept "Customer is the King" and approaches existing customers to strengthen brand loyalty through innovative strategies using technology. Basically a CRM tool creates a simple consumer interface based on a set of facts that facilitates businesses understand and speak with clients in a scalable way. CRM is one way of helping your staff to use technology to effectively build customer relationships to grow your business and increase profitability. It encompasses all your business activities giving you a clear picture of in which way your business is heading, including contact management, income control, workflow processes, productivity and sales position.

Though CRM is generally referred to as a tool to woo customers, its advantages go beyond customer satisfaction. It can incorporate all aspects of your business such as HR, advertising and supply chain management. In fact, CRM streamlines many of your processes addressing the important question of why CRM is crucial for the success of an organisation. It can encompass the entire gamut of your business activity thereby contributing to the steady and prosperous growth of your business or organisation.

An Overview of Your Business and Your Clients: Simply stated CRM is a software tool for automating all your business processes to ensure you keep a close tab on all your activities. It is a single window of information on your clients or customers typically using the software interface known as online dashboard. With a click of a button you can review processes, check for mistakes or errors if any and if needed take corrective measures with an integrated approach combining inputs from traditional sources as well as online platforms. It can also help you forecast your future and help you reorient businesses or products to meet changing customer or market needs.

CRM for Multi-Tasking Roles: In today's business environment lot of information and data is collected through various sources such as salespersons talking to customers on the ground, technicians and technical persons talking on assembly or production floors, accounts generating relevant income and expenditure information, and at the customer level many customers may be sending you feedback or asking for information through person, online or mobile which means there is going to be a flood of information. A software tool such as CRM enables a business to streamline all this information and more significantly to analyse the information so that you do not allow anything to fall through the cracks. As much as automation in industry, the use of software automation such as CRM is slowly beginning to be an integral part of every business or organisation.

INTROSPECTION QUESTIONNAIRE

1. What are the qualities of a good salesman?

2. What is the difference between sales & marketing?

3. What is CRM strategy? How will CRM approach improve the business?

4. Why customer retention is important in every business?

5. "Digital Marketing" has superseded "Internet Marketing" in the current business world. – Define.

Chapter – 10

"Today we are working for tomorrow's (Business) success"

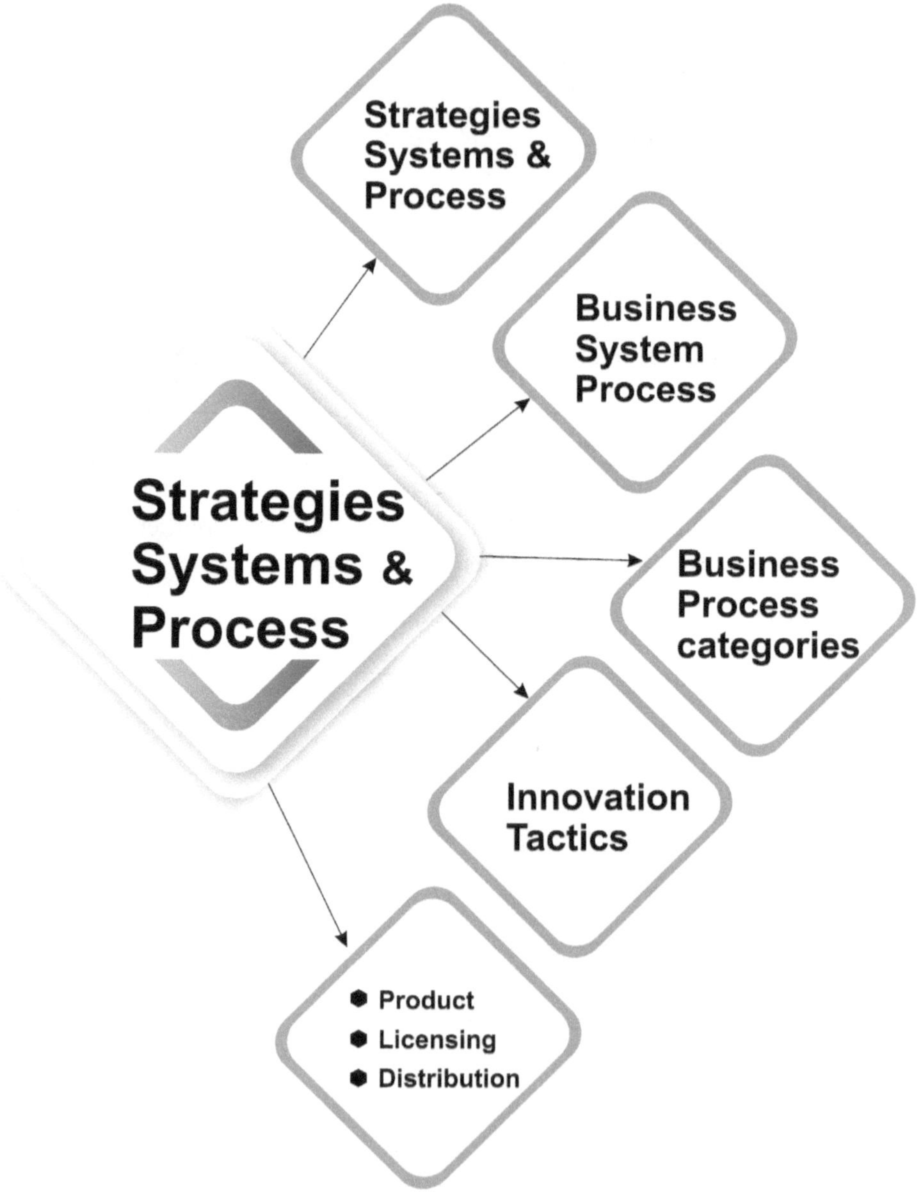

```
                    Strategies
                    Systems &
                    Process

                         Business
                         System
                         Process

Strategies
Systems &                     Business
Process                       Process
                              categories

                         Innovation
                         Tactics

              ● Product
              ● Licensing
              ● Distribution
```

Jyothi Reddy:

From a field labourer to a CEO of a US organisation, Jyothi Reddy own a US based software company with a vision to change lives in rural India.

Born in 1970, she was the second of 5 children in a poor family. As a result of the financial crunch of her family she was sent to an orphanage at an early age.

She was referred to as a motherless child to gain admission into the orphanage and she could never see her mother till she lived in the orphanage. Jyothi did not give up easily, she developed a strong will and worked towards shaping a better life as hardships taught values and an ability to think out of the box.

She studied in a government school while staying in the orphanage, then moved on to work and she lived in the superintendent's house and attended vocational training in tailoring. She was always looking for employment opportunities as early penury made her realise that financial empowerment was a must to be successful in life.

Jyothi was forced into marriage at 16 with her cousin and soon had 2 daughters. She was forced to take up a job as a farm labourer to make both ends meet and this further strengthened her resolve to fight harder in life.

Opportunity beckoned in the form of a government scheme called Nehru Yuva Kendra, which sought to create awareness among the youth. She became a volunteer and soon started teaching. The money was insufficient to run her family and she took to stitching at night and learnt typewriting too.

All through she had to battle socio-economic issues, but was undeterred. She pursued as well as completed a BA degree in 1994 and followed it up with an MA in 1997. This got her a job as a special teacher at a paltry of Rs. 398 per month. She had to travel 2 hours to reach the school and she utilised that time to sell saris to co-passengers to earn extra income. Her struggles of life made her time conscious and she used her time creatively.

Though her teaching job was regularised, she was not satisfied and visit from a relative who was in the US triggered dreams of going to the land of opportunities. Always hard working and multi-tasking, she learnt computers so that she could go to the US.

> Her initial days in the US were also a big struggle as she worked in a gas station and as a babysitter along with other odd jobs such as unloading and loading goods at a video store. Thanks to a close relative she joined CS America.
>
> Bus she soon had to get back to her gas station and babysitting jobs at which point of time she started thinking of doing something on her own. A visit to Mexico for visa stamping made her believe could start a consultancy as she was very familiar with the visa stamping process. She opened a consultancy office in 2011 with her savings of $40,000 and ensured her 2 daughters, whom she had left behind in India, joined her in the US to pursue their education.
>
> Now as a CEO of her own software company, Jyothi has a vision of empowering poor people in India and has been contributing to orphanages as well as old age homes.

I. STRATEGIES, SYSTEM & PROCESS

Approach, Company, Procedures and Systems:

System and Process are the important building blocks of our businesses. Each facet of your business or enterprise – on the shop floor, within the warehouse or in the workplace – is a part of a system that may be managed or improved by applying correct principles.

A business system is designed to connect all of an organisations' intricate elements and interrelated steps to work for the success of the business strategy.

When we apply defined principles and practices to the systems and techniques that deliver value to our customers, we are developing what is often referred to as a "business system."

Developing powerful business structures often unifies problem solving and decision making of the company. Many common tools and methodologies are universally taught and anticipated to be utilised at all levels. Numerous key management structures, which include a full-time performance excellence workplace or systematic maturity assessment, are made a permanent a part of the infrastructure. The business system also encompasses how we lead our staff and connect them to the operational method.

Why implement a business system? There are numerous reasons to put implement an enterprise system.

Enhancing Top-Line Performance: Part of the business system is the development and implementation of strategy creation, business methods and strategic planning. These are the foundations to ensure that your business proceeds in the right direction for top-line sales. In short, a business system takes care of your business' destiny. It ensures you meet your clients' expectations and enhances your brand, which are keys to developing a healthy business. If you adopt a systematic method, your business will have constant flow of information on areas that you need to improve to meet customer satisfaction.

Meeting Customer Satisfaction: If you use a scientific technique, your organisation will analyse measure, evaluate and test all possibilities of what your customers want and don't want. You may have consistent facts on areas that need to be improved and, even more importantly, you will start to recognise unmet wishes of customers. A business system is adopted to improve the image of the brand that your organisation proposes to sell your customers as well as in the eyes of your staff and suppliers.

Consistent Results: Whether or not you are considering safety, quality or getting the work done in a timely manner, a business enterprise is designed to give you effective and repeatable results.

Employee Engagement: The goal of the system is to enable proper education and opportunities to all employees so that they will complete their work extra efficiently and effectively. We also seek to harness their ideas and creativity and, in the process, increase their personal engagement. Moreover, having the system in place permits you to integrate new-hires, and makes it easy for them to understand their role and contribute meaningfully for the growth of the organisation.

Reduce Cost and Increase Profits: it has been proven again and again that the implementation of a sound business system helps reduce costs. A business system is intended to reduce costs without taking shortcuts that often lead to an erosion of profitability because of the necessity to lower quality expectancies or service levels. Some organisations use performance excellence, among other things, to create a business system taking a holistic approach that includes the whole company. All pieces must fall in place to paint a picture that every employee will understand clearly. The business system based on performance excellence contains 4 components:

- **Approach:** The way in which the organisation thinks and plans.
- **Methods:** The way in which the organisation operates.
- **People:** The way in which the organisation leads.
- **Generation:** The way in which the organisation connects.

Without a business system in place different groups of an organisation work in their isolated zones. Each department would possibly be performing excellently well, but the combined results of a holistic approach don't reach customers. A business system focuses on the alignment of all aspects of a business organisation and presents a comprehensive end solution to the customer or client.

Approach: The success of a business system doesn't work on whims, it calls for careful thought and planning. A key factor of business system planning entails improvement and implementation of precise strategies, which ought to be a part of a written business plan that you create when starting your business. Successful business strategies encompass regions, inclusive of advertising, minimising costs, receiving reimbursement and persevering with training to meet changing market scenarios.

Negotiate: Small businesses normally don't have funds to spend lavishly on business systems along with office area, advertising campaigns or meeting other needs, so it important to become a good negotiator to ensure you get value for money. In case you're purchasing advertising space ensure that you get the best value for the amount you pay.

Self Development: Businesses need to continuously focus on self development to remain relevant in emerging markets. Make sure you diligently allocate funds for self development of your business practices, including your staff. This can be in various forms, including attending seminars or programmes as also deputing your staff to attend such programmes on a continuous basis.

Trumpet Your USP: At the very outset recognise the USP of your product or business and trumpet it in all your advertising campaigns be it direct, indirect or online. This can give an edge over your competition and attract more prospective customers or clients to your product or business.

Get the Right Price: Pricing a product or service or seeking a commission for a service done can be a tricky task. Make sure that you get the right price for your goods or services without impacting customer relations. Give deep thought to your pricing patterns even as you evolve your business plan.

Avoid Unwanted Expenses: Cutting costs by avoiding unwanted costs such as getting into court litigations can protect your bottom line. If you are into manufacturing, sometimes it will make sense to outsource projects rather than investing in a huge work force, especially if you have one-time or short-term orders.

Business Structure: How a business organisation is structured will depend on whether it is a small business or a big business. Small businesses generally can be structured in a simple manner with staff taking up multi-tasking roles. Big businesses, however, will have layers of structures to ensure the smooth functioning of the organisation. Small or big, all cogs will have to fit properly to ensure that the machine functions smoothly.

Fulfilling Ambitions: Initial ambitions are sparks for business dreams, big or small. But the ambitions and dreams need to be spelt out clearly focussing on every minute detail from finances, infrastructure, staffing, product to automation process be if manufacturing or using of relevant software. While small businesses may largely focus on finances and outputs be it retail business or manufacturing, big businesses will have to focus on the overall large picture to ensure ambitions and dreams are fulfilled.

Corporate Procedure: A systemised procedure with defined roles to ensure that work goes on with clockwork precision to fulfil the dream of the entrepreneur who ventured into the business. Every minute plan needs to be worked out in the business system or the enterprise system in a step by step manner defining goals and means of achieving them. It may also be necessary to reorient business plans to meet changing market dynamics.

Corporate Records: Data collection and analysis, especially in today's technology driven world, is an ongoing process. Bigger the company, the higher the data collection and analysis. Depending on the size of an organisation, appropriate systems will have to be implemented or incorporated to maintain all forms of data, which has to be secured and at the same time be accessible for key members of an organisation.

Constraints: Despite the best of plans, a business or organisation can run into hurdles, some expected and some unexpected. Take for example for a small business, the availability of funds can be a constraint till such time as the business or product starts making a viable profit. Similarly, when a business or an organisation is dependent on systems such as manufacturing equipment or software solutions along with requisite hardware systems, there can be some unexpected hurdles or constraints. It is always good to focus on back up plans and allocate financial resources to overcome hurdles or constraints.

Right Inputs: As soon as the planning process has integrated all ideas into information systems, it is critical to ensure the involvement of end users in the interface. Bank on the expertise of individuals who can carry out the task by providing the required information with a view to ensuring that the focus is on end user, who is important to for the success of your business plan. Even when putting a system into place there is always the dilemma if inputs are too much or too less. Individual experts may tend to input too much of information, so it is essential to provide the right inputs for whatever systems you create.

Implementation: Yes the implementation of any business plan is the most crucial for the success of any business organisation. Just jotting down a dream and expanding it into a perfect plan will not be sufficient. The plan will also have to be implemented to near perfection because nothing is 100 percent perfect in today's world. Giving margins for errors, your business plan needs to be implemented with proper delegations of tasks and assignments. The successful implementation of your business plan with the right business system in place will surely be the key to the success of your business or organisation.

Examples of Business Systems and Processes:

- Lead Generation
- Customer service
- Buying
- Income Conversion

- Hiring
- Inventory control
- Internet site
- Schooling
- Transport
- Pricing
- Accounting
- Information systems
- Operations
- Payroll
- Protection
- Order success
- Collections
- Custodial

Having an effective business system is the practical way to manage important details of your operation. These details are observed in lower-stage sub-systems. For example, your advertising and marketing system can also have a subsystem referred to as lead generation. The lead generation system ought to have sub-systems consisting of mail, telemarketing, or radio advertising. Systems and sub-systems are the workhorses that provide consistent results, even while you are now not around.

A business system can be as simple as a checklist created in an hour or two. However, extra complex systems can take days or maybe weeks to put into effect. The best systems consider such factors as design, components, people, quality, speed and dimension.

There are "best practices" for creating high-performance business systems and processes that pay big dividends when applied correctly.

Formula for Success: Good systems take waste and inefficiency out of your business and help you give customers or clients what they want, every single time. They are the solution to low business income, low-profit margins, patron dissatisfaction, overall negative sentiments, employee turnover and every day frustration. Good systems also help you overcome business hurdles so that you sustain your credibility as well as accountability to focus on customer satisfaction and improving your profit margins.

Create systems in such a manner that they continue to sustain your organisation irrespective of who is there are not. Yes, you require human resources to run systems, but systems can be permanent while there can be a turnaround of human resources. Take a leaf out of global business practices and adapt them to suit your local needs.

In fact if you look at the most successful global business brands or organisations, be it food chains, Information Technology companies, international courier services or retail marketers, they thrive because they recognised early in their endeavours to set-up fool proof systems to sustain their business activities on a long-term basis irrespective of the geography from which they operated.

Business System Process: Setting up a business system starts with outlining goals and ends with achievement of the business objective of providing customer satisfaction. It can additionally incorporate all other aspects of your business with the ultimate aim of making your dream business a success. The key components of a business system can comprise:

1. **Operational Tactics:**

    These concern day-to-day operations also involving your staff and interactions with clients covering all facets of manufacturing, showcasing or retailing, selling and buying. This will identify operational roles of staff as well as their responsibilities in executing your business plan and achieving targeted results.

2. **Management Tactics:**

    Depending on the size of the organisation, this encompasses the decision making and conveying process of the top management on all governance issues such as budget and finance. This is to ensure that the right decisions are taken by the right people at the right time for the smooth functioning of your business or organisation.

3. **Assisting or Supporting Tactics:**

    This deals with human-related matters such as staffing pattern, recruitment, training process and other employee-related matters.

This can be an ongoing process to ensure that all compliances are met and all gaps be it staffing, sourcing or retailing are met to ensure a hitch-free operation.

In bigger organisations the business plan can be a little more complex and divided into sub-processes. But the big picture plan will be to map all the processes in such a manner that efficient results are obtained with the right coordination of the various elements of the sub-processes. The idea of sub-dividing is to ensure right controls at different levels of the big organisation with the single object of taking the business or the organisation to the height of success.

Like any plan or strategy, business process also needs to be reviewed and revamped periodically. Certain set norms may need to be changed to meet new challenges or changing market scenarios. Depending on the type and size of the organisation, the process can be reviewed to remove redundant portions and make sure that plans and processes are aligned with the current situation of the business or organisation.

Business Process Categories:

Depending on the organisation, business and nature of labour, business process methods are normally divided into 3 categories:

Operational or Primary Process: This deals with the core business of the organisation, including taking orders and delivering services or products to customers. This process addresses operational strategies and how a business is going to deliver the ultimate customer satisfaction.

Support Process: This does not directly deal with customers but addresses matters relating to how the business is going to work towards providing it send product or services. In short, it works on the route map for delivery of products or services through a work flow system.

Management Process: This is the back end or the backbone of how a business is going to be run and will depend on the nature of the organisation. It basically encompasses governance issues including strategic planning, budgeting and infrastructure building or enhancement. This does not have a direct bearing on the customer.

Progressive Merchandise & Strategies: Innovation to grow business with markets at all levels being competitive be it local, national or global, innovation by exploiting new ideas is crucial for the growth of a business and increasing profitability of a business venture or organisation.

Given below are some tips on how to innovate business practices:

- Business case for innovation
- Approaches to innovation
- Planning innovation
- Encourage innovation for your enterprise
- Funding innovation

Business Case for Innovation: It is absolutely essential to be clear about the difference between invention and innovation. While invention is a brand new concept, while innovation is creatively turning around existing business situations to overcome challenges either existing or perceived. Innovation can be at every single step of the business process such as providing customers with a product that has a feature that is different from similarly existing products. Innovation can also be a step in the existing processes that can reduce your costs. Innovation can also be providing some form of training for your staff to handle customers in a more proactive manner. Innovation is adding a new value chain to your system, processes or organisation which can give new insights to you, your staff as well as your customers. Innovation can also be in the sales and marketing processes or promotional activities such as using new online platforms, providing out of turn incentives or anything that draws the attention of customers to your business, product or organisations.

Introducing Innovation Can Help You to:

- Improve productivity
- Reduce costs
- Be more competitive
- Build value for your brand
- Establish new partnerships and relationships
- Increase turnover and enhance profitability

Organisations that fail to innovate run the risk of:

- Losing market share to competitors
- Falling productivity and efficiency
- Losing key staff
- Experiencing steadily reducing margins and earnings
- Going out of business

Innovation Tactics:

Analyse the Market: There is no point considering innovation in a vacuum. To take your business forward, observe your market and recognise how innovation can be advantageous to your clients or customers.

Areas for Innovation: You could identify possible areas for innovation of your business or product from the results of the market analysis. Either you can launch a new product or make subtle changes in existing product that can meet market demands – the automobile industry can be one example where manufacturers need to concentrate on meeting non-polluting standards as envisaged by governments. Software is another area where constant updates are a form of innovation to make the product better and user friendly. With online marketing and home delivery becoming popular even in tier 2 cities, you can possibly explore how your business or organisation can tap these marketing processes. In a competitive market, instead of undercutting prices of products to beat the competition try to provide something unique which makes your product standout from the rest of similar products.

Ideas for Innovation: Some innovative ideas may occur to you on the spur of the moment, but innovation has to be a constant part of your business plan. It is a general tendency to seek innovation in one aspect of a business venture such as a product or service, but you can stand out in the crowd if you include innovation in every aspect of your business endeavour. You can also encourage your staff to come up with creative and innovative ideas in the larger interest of improving your profit margins.

Study Your Competitors: Keep a close eye on your competitors and try to get as much information as you can get about their practices from all sources available in the market, including their advertising and marketing strategies.

If you find your competitor is focussing on a particular aspect to attract clients or customers, you can then think of the other aspects of a product or service to promote it as your USP. Keeping a close watch on your business environment will help you come up with innovative ideas. Apart from advertisements, you can approach news media to write advertorials highlighting your business or business practices to get that bit of extra mileage.

Develop a Rapport with Your Customers or Consumers: Customers or consumers can also be a great source of innovative ideas for you once you gain their confidence and build a rapport. You can perhaps organise a small contest – offline or online – asking customers or consumers what they expect from your business. Reward the best ideas and strengthen your consumer or customer base.

Involve Other Vendors and Stakeholders: Any business does not occur as a standalone activity. It involves other vendors and stakeholders, occasionally it will be great to seek inputs from them also on what they think can be one of your best innovative practices. Vendors deal with other similar businesses and can give some insights on how you can be better or innovative.

However, before implementing any innovation, you can ask yourself:

- What impact will the innovation have on your business or product?
- What additional human resource will you need?
- What other resources will you need to pool?
- How are you going to fund the innovation?
- With this innovation will you be creating something proprietary that will require copyright registration?

Some steps to Seek Innovative Ideas:

- Make sure you have a suggestion box prominently displayed in your business organisation to encourage customers/clients to come up with new ideas.
- Encourage your staff to participate in brain storming sessions to come up with new thoughts and ideas.
- Create a supportive atmosphere in which staff members feel free to express their thoughts without the fear of being ridiculed.

- Don't be overbearing on staff if they come up with some unusual crazy thought.

- Stress on team work among your staff, encourage them to discuss and also ask them to tap other resources to come up with innovative thoughts.

- Without being hierarchical make it comfortable for staff at all levels to speak openly without fear of reprisal. If a staff or a customer come up with a really novel idea that worked for your business or product, reward them suitably. This will encourage others to follow suit.

- When recruiting new staff at the very outset try to find out if they have any new ideas on the business or service that you are offering.

Funding Innovation: The success of any business development activity will hinge on the availability of adequate funding. Depending on the size of the business or organisation, funding can be tapped from various sources. At the outset when you launch your business, you can earmark certain amount for such activities. Other external sources can be from banks or financial institutions provided you have a strong business and action plan as well as justify to the investor that your innovation plan will reap rewards. Sometimes big companies go for public issues to fund future growth based on innovation or sometimes some businesses, especially in the Information Technology segment, bank on angel investors or venture capitalists. Sources are available but you must make the right noises to tap them.

Forms of Innovation:

The general impression when one talks of innovation is the launch of a new product. A new product can be innovative, but innovation in a business can take other forms also including innovation of an existing product.

Product Innovation: A product innovation is called for when you find that your product or service is getting stagnated in the market. Your product or service may have value but for some reason is not attracting attention of customers, maybe because the competition has done something better. You can put your thinking cap on and come up with some subtle changes or innovation so that you recapture the market by attracting customers – old and new – again.

Licensing Innovation: This is a good method to generate reasonably good income by riding piggyback on the brand of an established business or organisation. As a licensee of a well-known brand, you refurbish the image of your own business or organisation, but will have to meet the standards of the licensor to ensure that you keep your reputation intact.

Distribution Innovation: Another area of business merchandising to ensure reasonable profit is to take up distribution of well-known brands, this especially works well in the garment segment where a retailer can stand out by showcasing brands that his competitors may not have. If you are a manufacturer, you can piggyback on the label of a brand by outsourcing your products to that brand. If you maintain standards as desired by the brand, you are sure to sustain a steady business and income.

INTROSPECTION QUESTIONNAIRE

1. What is system & process in a business firm? Why is it important?

   _____

   _____

2. What is negotiation in a business and what would you gain out of it?

   _____

   _____

3. Why should your product be innovative in the current market?

   _____

   _____

4. What is the market threat expected, if your product is not innovative?

   _____

   _____

5. What is cost-cutting in a business and how will it improve the profit margin?

   _____

   _____

Chapter – 11

"The Result you achieve will be in direct proportion to the Effort you apply"

EFFORTS & RESULTS

- Effective Execution Excellence
- *Focusing on* **Efforts & Results**

Ramesh Babu – Hair Stylist Who Owns a Rolls Royce:

His core business is hair cutting and hair styling. An ordinary businessman, but with extraordinary wealth. How so?

He owns a fleet of 67 different kinds of cars.

Life was never easy for Ramesh Babu. He was 9 when his father passed away leaving behind a legacy of a hair cutting salon.

His mother worked as a cook to feed her children and get them educated. She had hired the salon on a rental basis.

Growing up on a meal a day tugged at his heart strings and he was divided between continuing to study and taking up a job to support his family.

His mother insisted that he continues to study to obtain a basic degree. He, however, decided to pursue his father's business of running the hair cutting salon.

He renamed the shop Inner Space. He realised his dream of owning a car when he purchased a Maruti Omni. He rented it out and soon his passion for cars turned into a successful car rental business.

In 2004, he established a luxury self drive car rental business in the newly opening segment of the tourism sector. Ramesh Tours and Travels has since not looked back. But Ramesh Babu still works in his saloon as he doesn't want to lose touch with his true roots. He has special clients who come only to his salon for hair styling. Ramesh has taught hairstyling skills to his children and wants to ensure the salon always runs successfully. He does not take any day off except during family trips.

EFFORTS

I. Effective Income:

Customers' purchasing decisions keep changing constantly, which means you have to reorient sales strategy with your staff. It takes some amount of persuasion to convince a customer to buy a product, but you have to step very carefully when being persuasive. Neither you or your staff can be smug or ordering customers keeping in mind that a satisfied customer will most likely come to your business or organisation again. Some useful tips on making a sales pitch:

Pick Out the Choice Maker: Customers are as varied as your product range, so you have to hit the right chord to make sure you keep them satisfied. With careful observation, you can pick the choice maker among your customers to make your pitch. Sometimes customers may listen to you but will depend on someone else to make the choice. So if you make pleasant conversation with the choice maker and make that person happy, you are likely to benefit with good sales.

Be True: Sales pitches can tend to get drowned in over exaggeration, so it is pertinent to give your customer the right information. As a salesperson you should be prepared to answer a plethora of questions, make sure either you or your sales staff are trained to know answers to questions that customers may ask about your product or service.

Create a Sense of Urgency: One of the tactics of a good salesperson is to create a sense of urgency among customers by saying certain deals are available only for a limited period of time. You can politely steer your customer to buying your product or service by creating a feeling that they would miss out on something big if they do not make the choice soon.

Win Over Objections: Some tough customers need to be handled with care especially when the raise objections to your pitch. Instead of getting caught off guard, it will be good to be prepared beforehand. This will require patience and preferably an experienced staff member can be specifically assigned to handle such customers.

Recognise Your Opposition: Comparisons are going to be a daily part of your business or sales activities as customers always tend to compare products or services. So you and your staff need to be aware of or educated about your competition and also be prepared to effectively counter comparisons from customers. Listen to your customer and reply to them convincingly, it will go a long way in ensuring profitable businesses.

Watch What You Say: Needless to stress any number of times that the 'Customer is the King,' so it is always good to make sure to watch what you say, never get into a situation where you put your foot into your mouth.

II. Significance of Effective Sales:

A large business need not necessarily have a large sales force, rather today the focus is on recruiting talent who can effectively ensure sales conversions from prospective buyers. With high competition and low returns due to various factors, it is imperative for businesses and organisations on finding the right talent and training staff on effective sales to boost income-generating resources.

Informing and educating yourself and your sales as well as marketing teams about your products or services is a constant and ongoing effort. Similarly creating the right content for advertising your product through media channels is also important and challenging as today technology provides for creation of ample advertising pitches for both you and your competitor. Overall there is need to create the right content for your offline and online sales pitches as well make sure they are easily accessible. With a big information explosion, salespersons may get confused about picking the right information and material. Any information in physical form would mean additional storage space, which can today be solved by availing of online cloud platforms. But make sure that you and your sales people or who else needs to access the information regularly are well trained to know how to handle the online resources.

Reviewing Your Performance: Every once in a while it is good to review your performance in terms of the efforts that you have put and what returns you have achieved for the same. While business successes can be driven by personal perceptions, the common notion for judging the success of a business or organisation is in terms of revenues generated and profit earned. You cannot achieve success in the long-term without hard work, the harder you work the greater will your success rate be. Along with hard work you have to keep a tab on all aspects of your business or organisation to ensure everything is working smoothly to meet your avowed business goals resulting in revenue and profit.

How to Periodically Measure Your Success?: The most common method of evaluating success is based on quarterly performance results of a business or organisation. The comparison of the quarterly results shows how a business is sustaining its margin or whether it has suffered some loss. This helps the management to come up with remedial measures wherever needed and also makes the management come up with future projections. Another interesting way of evaluation is on a yearly basis wherein you can compare your performance over 2 corresponding years to see where your business stands in terms of revenue, profit or future projections. It will help you assess if you have met projected targets or any course correction is needed for the next annual appraisal period.

Typically when you look at a business growth chart, you begin at the bottom of the graph and slowly over a period of time rise up to the level of success that you had determined or even perform better than expected. By creating a graphic chart of your quarterly or annual business performances, you get a clear picture of what the situation is in terms of revenue generation or profits earned. There could be some ups and downs in your graphic chart for example higher revenue generation need not necessarily mean increased profits as your expenditure could have risen due to some known or unknown reasons. When businesses begin to grow and managements invest in skilled or qualified human resources, the owners or stakeholders tend to withdraw from routine daily activities in order to focus on other issues to make sure that their business, product or organisation is on the right path. Irrespective of intentions or size of the business, it will be good to have a graphic chart of your performances on a quarterly and annual basis to know exactly in which direction you are heading.

Focussing On Efforts & Results: I am a big believer in setting goals, which lead you in the right path to achieve success in your business or organisation. Once you get into the goal setting habit, it can be categorised into short-term, mid-term and long-term. Setting goals is a good way to start your business or organisation as it leads to the roadmap of your success. With a set purpose in mind, it becomes easier to focus on 100 per cent efforts so that you can achieve your business dream. With 100 per cent efforts you really work hard, motivating your team small or big to follow suit.

Hard work ultimately is the route to success and if you are doing it with honesty and integrity it can really help you achieve your business goals. You work hard giving out all your best and keep faith that your honest efforts will be rewarded. But whatever big picture goal or aim you have, you have to work on achieving it frame by frame, which will in turn be the shorter and mid-term goals. An example outside of business is how a person wants to get a good job with a good salary and comforts of life by working hard and climbing the ladder of success step by step.

That is a big picture goal, but in order to achieve it, that person will have to fulfil short-term goals of getting a good and appropriate education, followed by a mid-term goal of getting a job with decent salary and work her or his way up to reach the ultimate goal of life of comfort. Thus any business with a big picture first needs to fulfil the smaller or short-term and mid-term goals.

Even if there appear to be some setbacks, you should continue to pursue because your goal setting and process that you adopt to achieve the goals will also evolve methods to overcome stumbling blocks. So sustained efforts based on goals is a crucial key to the success of a business or an organisation.

How to Specialise in Achieving Goals, Given Below Are a Few Tips:

Focus On Your Goals Forget the Outside World: It is indeed tempting to compare and look at what competitors are doing – it is good to have an eye on competition, but you must focus on your set goals and work on achieving it. Use whatever methods that suit you to achieve your set goals, but pursue it with honesty not worried about what others do or think about what you do and surely you will be on the road to success.

Encourage Experimentation: Sometimes doing things differently or experimenting will give good results. So be open to new thoughts or ideas and try them out when suggested by family, friend or staff. You likely may stumble on a best practice for your business or organisation.

Enjoy What You Do: This is the biggest key to success in any walk of life, to enjoy what we do. You have ventured to become a businessman, make sure you enjoy every moment of your business activity. Your business and life make take you in different directions, but make sure you don't lose focus or enjoy your work.

Stay On Top Always: As an owner of an organisation or a business, you have to be on top of every situation. Whatever influences you come under, be sure that you are the decision maker. Be the leader and lead with example to ensure that your staff, customers, suppliers or any other stake holder respects you for being the right leader and contributing to the success of your business.

Don't Be Complacent with Your Success: Success at times can also have a negative impact on your business or organisation especially if you tend to get content with your profit margins. It will lead to complacency and in the long run it can impact your business or organisation. So while good profits or results are the most significant aspects of your business, make sure to focus on your efforts, your goals or your plans with a view to improving constantly so that you don't fall in the complacency trap.

Be Confident: The success of any business or organisation that you want to start will also stem from how confident you are. You have given up a job, have a business plan, have all goals set, have the necessary infrastructure in place or getting ready, but be very confident that you will achieve your goals. Never let even an iota of doubt to creep into your mind and broadly carry confidence on your shoulders to achieve your business dream.

Even when you make efforts, you need to have some procedures to follow in place:

- At the outset, don't look at profits immediately. Focus on your efforts as per your goals and plans diligently, rewards will follow.
- Stop worrying about what others will think about your overall performance.
- View every attempt as a stepping stone for the next attempt.
- Put yourself in your customers' shoes and choose the right rates for your products or services in such a way that you are the winner. Take solace in your victory or victorious moment when there is a down turn, don't let frustration seep in. Sustain your business with your best practices.
- Recognise the fact that there are going to be good times and bad times in your business or organisation. With experience and determination, you will learn to get over the consequences of a bad time. Rejuvenate with fresh energy to overcome any crisis or difficult situations.

RESULTS

Business activity is a team game and as a leader of a business or organisation you need to strike the right balance to take your staff/team members along to meet your larger goals. Some tips are given below:

Saying Inspiring Words: Motivating colleagues or staff helps build a good team effort, this can be achieved by saying a few words of inspiration when a staff member does something good. A little word of praise will give confidence to your staff that you care for them and are aware of their contributions to their success however small it is.

Deploy the Right Human Resources for Tasks On Hand: Your staff may have different skills, make sure that you position the right staff for the right jobs so that you can utilise their capacity to maximum. Knowing the strengths and weaknesses of your staff and deploying them to exploit their strengths will help you achieve your goals along with your sustained efforts.

Resolve Issues Together: If some issue in your business or organisation needs to be resolved, make sure that you get inputs from your staff also. Even if it is planning some strategic change, getting inputs will help evolve a good plan as well as make your staff feel a sense of belonging. A few staff may be outspoken, but make sure other employees also get a chance to share their views.

Recruit the Best: Recruiting the right staff is as important as deploying the right personnel for the best use of human resources. At the very outset be polite and open in your conversations with potential candidates during recruitment so that you can recruit the best possible candidates to suit your business or organisation needs.

Balance Work and Fun: As an owner of a business or an organisation, you will have to keep your staff in good humour to extract the maximum effort out of them. You can't load them with too much of work, which can burn them out, nor can you allow them to have too much of fun. Ensure there is a right balance to break the monotony and keep your staff in health spirits.

Maintain Stability: A stable work force is like a strong backbone of any organisation and they can contribute immensely to the success of any organisation. Ensure your human resources are properly handled to ensure stable growth of your business or organisation.

INTROSPECTION QUESTIONNAIRE

1. What is sales effectiveness?

    _____

    _____

2. Effort vs Results in an organisation – define with a few examples.

    _____

    _____

3. How will you face objections in the market and the ways to overcome them?

4. As a leader in this competitive world, how will you be different to your customers comparing to your competitors?

5. Define what is gap analysis in a business.

Chapter – 12

*"You don't develop a business,
You develop a team, the team will develop the business"*

Corporate Education & Team Building

— Training Needs & Methods

— Team Building activities

**Educate, Develop
&
Delegate the Team**

— Delegating work

— Handling Expertise

— Replacement Plans

Practice it as a Routine

Nitin Godse – Excel Gas & Equipment Company:

From a poor family based in Akole village of Ahmednagar in Maharashtra, Nithin Godse wanted to become an engineer. However, he had to settle for a BSC degree. After graduating, he got a job as a supervisor and saved money to study MBA. In fact, his early life was such a struggle that he had to work as a labourer and sell vegetables to support his family.

On completing MBA, he worked day and night for an agro-based start-up. He then decided to channel his energies into following his passion and starting his own business.

With investment from a relative, he started the Excel Gas and Equipment Company in 1999. The venture has grown to become a one stop solution for all gas piping projects. The business expanded to the Middle East with an impressive client base.

Ranked among the top 5 on site tubing and piping installations, supplying of services onsite and subcontracting, the company has a turnover of Rs. 50 crores and employee strength of 200.

EDUCATE, DEVELOP & DELEGATE THE TEAM

The Significance of Corporate Training in Team Building:

Education of employees doesn't stop at school or colleges, it rather begins in your business or organisation. Any successful business or organisation will look forward to its employees learning continuously as an ongoing process. Individuals too look forward to learning opportunities to enhance their skills and grow in an organisation. So as a business or organisation you will need to look for trainers, in-house or external, to constantly upgrade or hone skills of your staff. These trainers are not just people who give delusional speeches to large groups, instead they are skilled professionals who have the ability to train your staff to improve your overall business.

Enhancing or Inculcating Professional Skills:

Corporate trainers focus on enhancing professional skills rather teaching academic knowhow. Based on the specific needs of your organisation or business they will impart needed skills to improve their efficiency and contribute towards the growth of your business or organisation. The trainers can either inculcate professional skills for an industry or inspire your staff to be better communicators, especially when dealing with customers or working as a team. This can sometimes be challenging for the trainer as some employees may inadvertently tend to resist learning something new. It is not that they are reluctant but somewhere inside there is a mental block, which needs to be cleared. So corporate trainers evolve different methods including evolving simple games or team building activities so that the fun element makes the exercise worthwhile for your staff and the trainer.

The Role of a Corporate Trainer:

A corporate trainer is a specialised person who can be part of an in-house team or can be someone who is hired on contract for specific training schedules. At the outset, a corporate trainer needs to an excellent communicator, who can engage with large audiences in a very effective manner and retain their attention for long periods of time. A corporate trainer needs to know her or his subject thoroughly well as they can easily be exposed by career professionals, especially if they are dealing with mid-level employees. Normally corporate trainers develop their own individual personalities and styles to keep audiences engaged. A corporate trainer is a person who has a strong success story behind him or her and that makes employees to look up to that person as a role model. In fact, a corporate trainer is a person who has evolved in a business or organisation over a period of time and has mastered many multi-tasking skills. So it takes long years of relevant experience and exposure to become a good corporate trainer.

How to Work On Team Building?:

A corporate trainer has the onerous task of emphasising the role of team work and team building. In order to make members of a team comfortable with each other and work in close coordination, a corporate trainer will chalk out group activities wherein each member of a group has to contribute for the success of the team. So as a corporate trainer you need to have the ability to be friendly and an aptitude for working in a cooperative endeavour. So a corporate trainer may initially start off as an assistant who helps in team bonding activities, which may include simple sports or fun activities. Over a period of time, that person evolves into a functional corporate trainer within an organisation or as an independent consultant.

Improving Group Performance:

What areas of training or improvement your team needs? The definition of a brilliant team is one which works with the highest level of efficiency and responds with lightning speed in all situations. If required team members will voluntarily back up for each other and make sure nothing falls through the crack. If your business team does not fit into the above description, be assured you can evolve them into such a group.

To build your team with appropriate training is essential irrespective of whether you are a group leader or not, and this does not apply only to new recruits. It is a constant process like any of your other systems to enhance capabilities and work towards achieving your goal.

If you are a small or medium-sized business or organisation, you can carry out the job of recruiter, trainer and team leader. You can learn skills as a part of your business initiative to don the roles. In case you work in a big organisation, the Human Resources And Personality Development Department will chalk out programs for training in order to build team bonding. If you are a supervisor then you are in a tremendous position to understand and perceive what training will be suitable to make your staff perform better and can coordinate with the Human Resources And Personality Development Department to chalk out such programs. Given below are some useful suggestions to help improve skills of human resources:

Figuring Out Training Needs: The toughest challenge in a business or organisation is to figure out skill enhancement training needs. Begin with the appraisal process which also incorporates the professional profile description of each employee and also observe them at work. You can also interact with them to find out if they have any specific needs based on their roles with which they fit into your scheme of goals. By reviewing individual performances and group outputs, you can arrive at training programs and schedules.

Seeking information from individuals and assessing their collective needs through a simple survey can give you the right focus on what type of training you need to chalk out, both for individuals and the group. Role based training will give you the best desired results instead of generalised programmes – for example training in use of Microsoft XL spreadsheet may be of use to a specific group of employees, so it will be pertinent to train only those employees on spreadsheet usage instead of making it a generalised training for all members of a business or organisation.

Selecting the Right Training Methods: Having assessed the right training needs for your staff, the next task will be to choose methods to suit individual needs, group efficiency and meeting the overall goals of your business or organisation.

One of the current business training models known as 70:20:10 method suggests that 70 percentage of learning occurs through experience, inclusive of each day's experience; 20 percent through discussions with other people along with training; and 10 percent through traditional training programmes.

On-the-job training has now become an important part of many business or organisations with either an experienced colleague or a traditional trainer donning the role of a mentor and scheduling the training programmes with fun elements.

Personal Engagement: While skill enhancement through training gives a broader perspective, in some specific case staff or employees have to be dealt with one-to-one basis. There could be some performance gaps, which may not necessarily be due to lack of training. In such cases sitting down with the employee and sorting out the problem issue can be an ideal solution. You will also get to understand certain issues about which you can take corrective measures in the long run. It can be a motivating session as well for a few employees who may feel a little de-motivated for various reasons. Having a conversation with such employees will clear the air and the net result will be an improved performance by filling the gap, which in turn will contribute to the overall goal of fulfilling your business aims.

Team Building Activities: Team building activities have to be modelled on what you want to achieve from the activities. Understand the strengths and weaknesses of a team, be critically aware of the training needs of your staff and diligently work out a programme, which can even be a nice day trip from outside the office. The spirit of bonding can work better when one is outside the pressure of office space and the setting is very informal. For example, if lack of communication is an issue that you want to address then you can select a physical activity that will require each member to speak and communicate. Indirectly you can suggest to your team members that this kind of communication needs to be an ongoing process even in the office in order to achieve better results. Or the activity that you choose can address problem-fixing issues working as a team.

Delegating Work: The most delicate task in a business or an organisation is delegating work to the team. You may be afraid of handing over your tasks and duties to someone else for fear of not achieving the desired results. But doing the task all by yourself may not be practical and also denies opportunities for your team to learn new abilities. As in any aspect of your business or organisation, plan the process of delegating tasks and give the right guidelines so that members of your team can handle the tasks in the manner you want to achieve results. When tasks are delegated properly and desired results are achieved, it definitely is a morale booster for your team members.

Learning the art of delegation promotes self belief within a group and is just one of the key abilities of managers who use a transformational fashion of leadership. This approach will assist you to connect with your team members, set clear goals and be an example of integrity and credibility. It allows you to develop a team that is noticeably influenced and consistently attaining its personal and shared goals.

Handling Expertise: Though your HR Department plays the role of identifying and recruiting talent, you as a manager may at times uncover individuals in your team with exceptional skills or talent. You can work with your HR Department to encourage that talent or skill to blossom by providing additional training or skill enhancement.

Replacement Plans: Despite your best efforts to retain talent, there will be some level of attrition. Hence you also have to work out plans to replace talent, which can also be from the existing work force. Sometimes key positions may require immediate replacement and you will have to make sure that your team members are quickly ready to fulfil that role. It is relevant to note that a strong team is not built overnight though sometimes a group of talented people may fall into a team at the same time. Even then it takes certain amount of time and effort to build a team. But at any point of time, your team members should be prepared for exigencies of people exiting an organisation and their need to fill the gap. This can be achieved by constant upgradation of skills and training programmes. You can also prepare members of your team for higher tasks by delegating roles so that they are prepared to handle situations which may not be a routine part of their daily chore.

Practice It as a Routine: Either as a business owner or manager, you have to constantly deal with human resources. So it is always good to be abreast of the strengths and weaknesses of your staff and make sure they get the requisite training. You can work on their weaknesses to ensure that over a period of time they get the grasp of the situation and will fit the roles in which you envisage them.

INTROSPECTION QUESTIONNAIRE

1. How can corporate training help employees?

2. Whether is it easy to mould a fresher or an experienced person in an organisation? Why?

3. What is team building? How will it help your business?

4. Why should you delegate work to your team members? Narrate its advantages as a team leader.

5. How would you differentiate between classroom training and on-the-job training? Which is more useful for employees?

Chapter – 13

"Time and communication are the keys to build relationships"

- Effective Communication Skills
  - Powerful Conversation capabilities
  - Self Discipline
  - Honoring the Commitments
  - 10 Fears to overcome while starting a Business

> **Ritesh Agarwal – OYO Rooms:**
>
> A technology network for budget hotels founded by college dropout, Ritesh Agarwal at the age of 18 has backing of over 700 hotels and several capital sources. He is the CEO and founder of the hospitality business and the app OYO Rooms. It is now a network consisting of 2,200 hotels in 154 cities across India. The monthly revenues amount to $3.5 million and with a staff strength of 1500.
>
> OYO is tipped to become a start-up unicorn and has raised $125 million from 7 investors. Many awards and accolades have been bestowed on Ritesh.

I. POWERFUL CONVERSATION CAPABILITIES

The ability to communicate correctly with superiors, colleagues and staff is crucial, irrespective of what industry you work in. In this online era, it is essential to develop proper communication skills to make the right impression through telephone conversations, email communications and social media chat. Good communication skills will help any business to prosper and as a staff member of an organisation it will enhance your visibility among seniors and management. Some of the keys to be a good communicator are:

Be a Good Listener: Being a good listener is an important key to being a good communicator. You have to practice intense listening skills as nobody will be interested to communicate with a bad listener. You cannot be just talking business and profits with another person without listening to her or his views or opinions. Sometimes it will help if you ask the other person to clarify what they say, especially when you are not able to follow the gist of their conversation. This will truly give the impression that you are listening to the other person as well.

Non-Verbal Communication: Non-verbal communication also helps convey crucial messages, non-verbal communications can be your body language in the form of gestures, facial expression, eye contact or voice intonation. An easy, open stance if you are standing or a straight sitting position with a pleasant tone will make for a good non-verbal communication pose. Similarly, you can make appropriate eye contact without appearing to stare at the other person. The body language is also a good indicator of how the conversation is going, for example if a person is speaking without looking you into the eye it may indicate that the person is uncomfortable with what she or he is saying, or even blatantly hiding the truth.

Be Audible and Concise: There is a proverb which says, "Brevity is the soul of wit!" So you have to be brief and concise in your communication. Either speaking on phone or in person make sure that you convey your thoughts in simple easy to understand sentences in the shortest possible time. Do not ramble on and on till the person listening to you gets totally bored and loses interest in the conversation.

Be Pleasant: Either talking to customers, colleague or staff, you have to be pleasant in your approach with a smile. A friendly disposition will help the other person to feel free and comfortable to converse with you. Even if it is an email communication, make sure it begins with a pleasant note or a personal matter such as, "I hope you had a wonderful weekend."

Be Confident: While being friendly and pleasant, you also ought to be confident of what you are saying. At the same time do not be overbearing with your views. Make sure that you are listening to and responding to the other person, especially if it is a customer.

Be Empathetic: Being empathetic to a customer, colleague or staff makes a big difference during a conversation. It surely demonstrates to the listener that you are giving that person attention and time to listen to whatever they are saying.

Be Open-Minded: Being open-minded and flexible makes for a good conversationalist. Even if you disagree with the other person, you can be amenable to listening to the other person's views.

Be Appreciative: Human beings want to be praised and this is a common tendency. When you are speaking to another person, if that person makes a valid remark or point or suggestion about your business or organisation, you can appreciate that person. Even while speaking on a phone or communicating through email you can make the right appreciative noises to keep the other person engaged with you in the conversation.

Focus On Feedback: Giving and receiving the right feedback gives a business or organisation an added advantage. As much as you push hard to sell your product or service, you will also have to be ready to receive feedback from the customers. Or within an organisation a positive feedback, may be just a "thank you" will go a long way in boosting the morale of employees. Similarly when you receive feedback make sure that you send the right responses, if necessary seek clarification if a customer has not made her or his intentions clear.

Choose the Right Medium: The medium of communication is as much important as the message that you want to convey. If you want to convey something with regard to an employee's performance, it will be best to do it in person though the task may sometimes sound unpleasant. Similarly, if you have to convey with busy higher-ups in your office, you have to choose the right form of communication such as email without trying to pressurise them under their already busy schedule. If you are dealing with a customer, then there is nothing better than a verbal communication.

II. SELF DISCIPLINE! HONOURING COMMITMENTS!

Discipline in any business or organisation is akin to discipline in personal life. For example, it is like eating an extra helping of warm fudge sundae and burning of the extra calories in a gym or at the very outset staying determined not to eat the extra helping. Businesses or organisations practicing discipline have always had higher degrees of successes than those falling for temptations. Some tips to inculcate discipline in your business or organisation resulting in level-head decisions that benefit you in the long run.

Understand Your Weaknesses: Despite setting goals and charting out plans, nothing is totally perfect in this world. There are bound to be weaknesses in a business or an organisation as much as we have weaknesses in personal life (such as even simple temptations for potato wafer chips). So to realise and understand your weaknesses, rather than brushing it aside as irrelevant, will help you to focus on business discipline.

Avoid Temptations: There is a proverb, "Out of sight, out of mind." So whatever temptations that may come in your business opportunities try and completely avoid them by keeping them out of sight. Once you are trapped in the pitfall of temptation, it will be very difficult to survive and rejuvenate. At the very outset may sure that you follow healthy business practices with fewer distractions in whatever form they may be.

Set Clear Priorities and Execution Plans: You have dreamt of being a business person, you have set goals and have plans to fulfil your dream.

Make sure that your priorities are right along with clear execution plans. Stay focussed on the right track so that you can achieve your set target in the right manner without tarnishing your image or the image of your business.

Develop Self-Control: As much as you practice self-control in your personal life, make sure that your business processes are also self-controlled. Be it you or your staff, make sure that you will not deviate or adopt short cuts to achieve your ends – as explained earlier avoid the gym by avoiding the temptation of extra helping. This will have to be practiced over a period of time and exposure as higher a business or organisation grows, bigger will be temptations.

Keep It Easy Through Simple Steps: Acquiring business self-control can appear to be daunting at the beginning, especially when you consider the large picture of your whole business mission. To avoid feeling intimidated, take small but easy steps recognising the immediate needs. It will soon grow into your entire business or organisation thus making it easy to avoid temptations.

Keep the Business Healthy: If your business has to be healthy, you and your staff need to be healthy. Avoid getting too excited at your office or business premises, try as much as you can to be cool even if the situation so warrants you to get tense. Make sure your staff follow the same principle.

Self Evaluate Your Ideas of Self-Control: Self-control comes out of self discipline, which in turn requires a certain amount of strong will power. So it will be good if you can self evaluate the strength of your will power in your business actions and slowly evolve it over a period time by practicing patience and perseverance, you will start gaining self-control in your business.

Have An Alternate Plan: Many things in business as in life are easier said than done. However we try had to discipline our business practices and follow a correct path, there could be some obstacles that may rattle you or distract you. So always have an alternate plan, like for example in personal life in order to avoid the temptation of something unhealthy you will end up sipping or chewing something. Similarly, when huge temptations confront you in your business, make sure that you have a substitute plan to avoid hurdles.

Praise Yourself: Once in a while you can pat your own back if you have achieved something more than the normal. The same applies to your staff in business or colleagues in your organisation. If you have a small business and have done exceptionally well praise the entire team for the good job done. This will be a great motivator in practicing discipline and self-control.

Forgive and Move Ahead: Even the best of plans can result in some failures. Quickly remedy the situation and move ahead. Don't focus too much on blame games, even if you are at fault don't hurt yourself too much. Again there is a proverb which says, "Failure is a stepping stone to success." Don't get trapped in guilt, anger or frustration as they can lead you further down the hill.

Honouring Commitments:

Business is all about meeting commitments, hence you should make sure that deadlines set for completing tasks are adhered to religiously. Every second counts when you decide to start a business or provide a service, the more prompt you are the better will be your success rate.

III. 10 FEARS TO OVERCOME WHEN STARTING A BUSINESS

Believe in the Good: A positive frame of mind makes for a good business or organisation. Having decided to chuck a job and start a business, make sure that you are in a positive frame of mind and will not succumb to any negative vibrations. Be it cost, infrastructure, resources or funding, stay positive in the fact that your business will follow a set process. At the very outset overcome the fear of negativity as even an iota of negative sentiments can hurt your prospects.

Threat Failure: Never harbour any thoughts of failure as you venture out to become a business person. You have made a conscious decision to venture out, stick to it at every turn of event based on your avowed goals. Never allow the fear of failure to creep in at any stage of your business plan implementation. You will surely encounter many "nos" along the path, but view every "no" as a new spark of opportunity. In short, walk the talk of your business plan without any thoughts on failure at any stage.

Failure of Returns: The ultimate aim of any business is return on investment or simply 'ROI.' This failure of generating sufficient returns for your investment can hanker at your mind. At the outset, you need to get rid of this desire of focussing on revenue or profit generation and work hard. You have to sustain your efforts with the strong view, returns will definitely come if you are doing the right business in the right manner.

Fear of Expansion: This is another area of concern for many businesses or organisations. Having reached a certain level, there is a dilemma of whether to expand or not. Don't allow this fear to nag your mind, instead think of how expansion plans can make your business more profitable. Basically, study the market and decide whether an expansion is needed or not. Depending on the results of the market survey you can take the right call.

Fear of Sustaining: Business sustainability is in your hands and you have to endure through all pains as well as climb the ladder of success step by step. Remain determined when things look to fall apart, drive away the fear of sustainability from your mind and continue to push the agenda of your business plan.

Being Passionate: Will being passionate about your work be an obstacle is a question that will arise in the minds of a businessman. Yes being passionate is definitely a positive step be it any profession. The more passionate you are about your business, the better will be your results.

Self Appreciation: The question is will self appreciation be seen as being vain. No you can appreciate yourself with a lot of self respect and that will induce a sense of confidence to take your business forward. Self appreciation can also wean you away from procrastination and you can be motivated to do better as you pursue your endeavour of fulfilling business dreams.

Dilemma of Dependency: When to delegate, whom to delegate, how to delegate, questions such as these can affect new entrepreneurs. Yes, delegation of work is definitely on the cards, especially if you have chalked out a good business plan, there is no need to fear about delegation of work to meet the end goals of your business or organisation.

Nurturing Relationships: Any business success depends on relationships both within the organisation and outside the organisation. So don't hesitate to focus on nurturing relationships be it with your customers, clients, staff or suppliers. At the very outset, you can hire the right people for your business to ensure the right relationships are nurtured resulting in the success of your business plan.

Seeking Opinions: Do I need to seek opinions, will it hurt my business interests? Seeking opinions from the right people will only enhance your business opportunities. Close associates, family, friends, staff or even customers can be opinion givers. Opinions can be ways of restructuring your business plans or overall goals, but the ultimate decision has to be yours. So take the best out of opinions, but be sure that the last mile decision is solely yours.

INTROSPECTION QUESTIONNAIRE

1. What is effective communication?
   _____
   _____

2. Why should you be a good listener?
   _____
   _____

3. What is open-mindedness?
   _____
   _____

4. Why should you honour your commitments in business?
   _____
   _____

5. What are anticipated threats in a new business? How will you overcome the same?
   _____
   _____

Chapter – 14

"The power of the man is in the power of the mind"
"Stay Committed to your Decisions, but stay flexible in your approach"

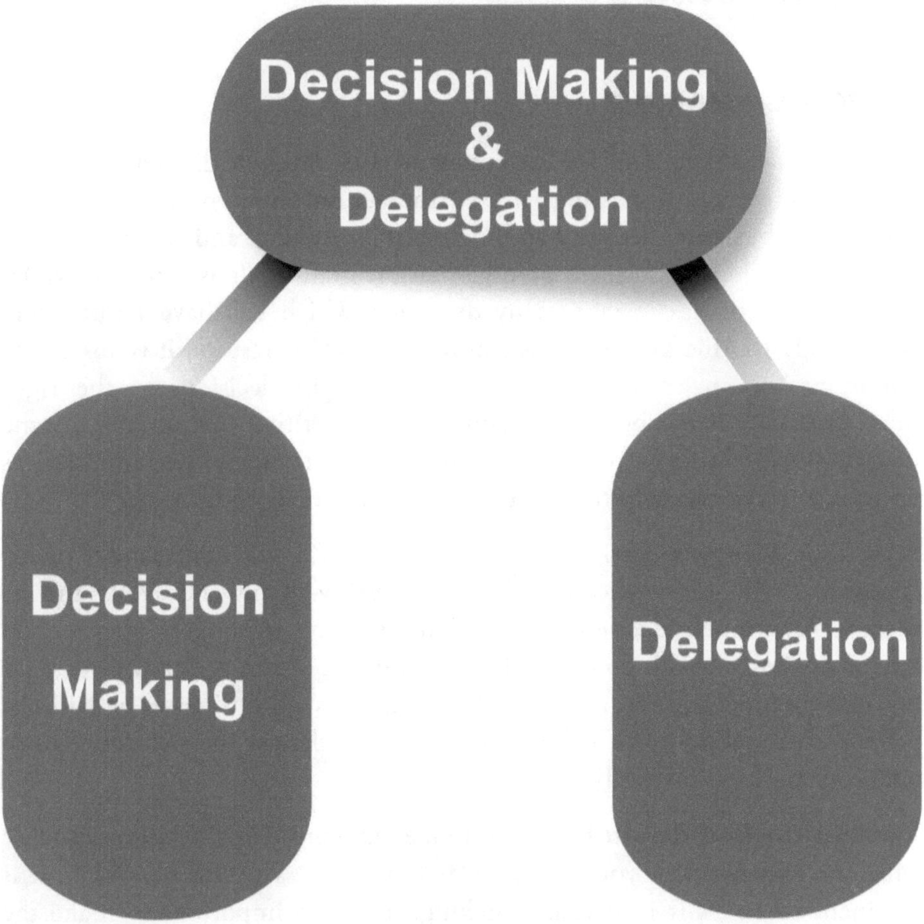

Decision Making & Delegation

- **Decision Making**
- **Delegation**

> **Kumaran Brothers – Go Dimensions:**
>
> Age is irrelevant when it comes to venturing into brand new start-ups has been proven beyond doubt by Shravan Kumaran (15 years old) and Sanjay Kumaran (14 years old).
>
> Running a company, Go Dimensions, since 2012 the brothers were identified as the youngest mobile application programmers in the world. Creating apps for iOS and Android, they developed over 11 and launched Windows apps too.
>
> Their only investment is buying gadgets for which they get ample support from their father Kumaran Surendran, who is in a senior position in Cognizant Technology Solutions.

I. DECISION MAKING

The everyday life style of an entrepreneur goes through different cycles of attending meetings, discussing with customers on phone or email, meeting day-to-day business needs, handling staff members and taking crucial decisions relating to business or organisation matters. It is a day in which the entrepreneur has to take many decisions, which will have a forbearing on his daily routine as well as his future business interest. So it is absolutely important for an entrepreneur to take the right decisions at the right time, especially if the business is run in a competitive environment. Some suggestions for business persons or entrepreneurs to make the right choices or decisions that can help them achieve success in their endeavours:

Seek Your Mentor's Advice: An entrepreneur is a sole commander of his enterprise. His quick actions outline the destiny of his endeavour and its success. And timely decisions are keys to reaching set targets or goals. So one of the best ways to go forward in this direction is to seek advice of your business mentor. You can also learn from similar such businesses or business persons and make sure that the decisions you make are the right choices to take your business forward.

Visualise the End Result: Before you take any considered decision visualise what the end result of your decision making process would be. While it is pertinent to be swift in decision making, it is also important to make the right decisions. Many successful entrepreneurs have indeed stressed on this point of how visualising the end result will help in making the right decision. So be a powerful decision maker by visualising the end result of your thought process to become a successful business person.

Learn from Others: Taking decisions through a thought process may take time to inculcate, but budding entrepreneurs can always look up to peers who have gone through such processes. So by studying successful entrepreneurs in the global scale, a prospective businessman takes cues that can help in the decision making process. An entrepreneur can also learn from successful business persons in the vicinity by personal interaction. Thus the process of taking right decisions can be a good learning curve from the experience of others.

Listen to Your Gut Feeling: To be a perfectionist is a tough call in today's complex world. But for an entrepreneur his intuition can also play a crucial role in making the right decision. After taking all aspects into consideration, listen to your gut feeling before making a choice.

II. DELEGATION

A prospective entrepreneur or business person will have to wear many hats during the day from a sales person, funder, CEO to innovator. Initially, this may look like fun, but as the business grows, it can tend to eat away lot of your time as you will also have to attend to day-to-day tasks. So it will make sense to think of delegating some of your tasks by recruiting the right talent so that you sustain your business enthusiasm over a longer period of time. Given below are some tips on delegating tasks on hand:

Force Yourself to Delegate: It is common for an entrepreneur to be possessive of his ideas and feel that delegation may not work. But an entrepreneur cannot carry the whole burden of his business set-up management. In order to ensure that you achieve maximum results, you have to make sure that you delegate some of your work so that it can work for the overall benefit of the organisation or the business.

Be Proactive: You proactively need to take the call on when you need to delegate some of the tasks. If you are going to wait till the last minute when you are on the verge of a burn out due to excessive tasks, then the idea may not work. So the moment you feel that work is piling up and you are not in a position to give sufficient time to all the tasks on hand, you need to recruit the right person to delegate some of the tasks. This can be done by listing out all the tasks that you need to do on an ongoing basis for the success of your business or organisation.

Understand Your Team's Strengths and Weaknesses: Once you set-up a team to carry your business forward, you need to quickly understand the strengths and weaknesses of each member of the team. This will ensure that you assign the right tasks to the right people so that your mission goals of a successful business are fulfilled.

Invest in Training: As a business decision maker, you should make sure that your team is trained to take up tasks. So after assessing their strengths and weaknesses, it will be good to set aside funds to train them to meet your expectations.

Explain Your Expectations Clearly: The best way to get the maximum out of your staff is to explain to them clearly what your expectations are. Give them a clear roadmap of what your goals are and how you see them fitting into your plans of achieving those goals. Devote time to clear their doubts and make it doubly clear that you have a vision and see a role for them to play in fulfilling that mission.

Trust But Check: While you need to have implicit trust in what your team members do, it will always be good to check if they are on the right track. After delegating a task, set realistic deadlines and monitor to make sure that they are working on schedule to meet the deadline. You can also monitor if they are following the right processes so that you can achieve the goal that you are aiming for. Establish open lines of communications so that your team members can be in constant touch with you, especially when they have some doubts to clear or questions to ask.

Provide and Obtain Feedback: While providing feedback to your team members on how they are performing on their delegated task, also make sure that they give you the appropriate feedback. This will give an indication of whether they are enjoying the tasks delegated to them or whether there are some issues in the processes, so that you can take corrective action. So by efficiently delegating work to the right people, you can achieve your goals in your chosen business domain.

INTROSPECTION QUESTIONNAIRE

1. How will you select your product for a new business in the current competitive world?
   _____
   _____

2. How will you recognise the strength and weakness of your team members?
   _____
   _____

3. How would you train a weak member in a team?
   _____
   _____

4. Why should you be proactive?
   _____
   _____

5. What is learning from mistakes?
   _____
   _____

Chapter – 15

"Assertiveness is not what you do, It's who you are!"

A　P　E　P
Attitude　Plan　Execution　Performance

1. Normal People vs Successful People

2.
★ Passive
★ Assertive
★ Aggressive

3. Assess your Communication Style.

4. Characteristics of Behavior.

> **King Siddharth – Createens:**
>
> Author, speaker and magazine publisher, King Siddharth has organised a teenage conference Createens. Young people will learn about blogging, entrepreneurship and much more from the expert at the conference.
>
> As a regular speaker of his designs and his philosophy, he explains why he dropped out and was never excited about formal education exited the learning curve.
>
> While at school and 11 years old, creative and confident King Siddharth organised events and ran his own show. Very creative and confident, he started an online publication called *Friend* to cater to like-minded people and developed an interest in filmmaking and shooting short videos.
>
> He gained significant knowledge in creating and designing websites. He worked on freelance projects and hired others to help him out in the projects.

APEP

A - Attitude
P - Plan
E - Execution
P - Performance

NORMAL PEOPLE

| ELIMINATE |  | ESSENTIALS |
| PREFER | | USELESS |

SUCCESSFULL PEOPLE

| ELIMINATE | ⟶ | USELESS |
| PREFER | ⟶ | ESSENTIALS |

TYPES OF ASSERTIVENESS

PASSIVE	ASSERTIVE	AGGRESSIVE
LONG, RAMBLING STATEMENTS	STATEMENTS THAT ARE BRIEF, CLEAR & TO THE POINT	EXCESS OF 'I' STATEMENTS
FILL IN WORDS (E.G. MAYBE)	'I' STATEMENTS: I'd like	BOASTFULLNESS: "MY"
FREQUENT JUSTIFICATION	DISTINCTIONS BETWEEN FACTS & OPINION	THREATENING QUESTIONS
APOLOGIES & PERMISSION SEEKERS	SUGGESTIONS NOT WEIGHTED WITH ADVICE	REQUEST AS INSTRUCTIONS OR THREATS
FEW 'I' STATEMENTS (OFTEN QUALIFIED)	NO SHOULDS OR OUGHTS	HEAVILY WEIGHTED ADVICE IN THE FORM OF 'SHOULD' AND 'OUGHT'
SELF PUT DOWNS (E.G. I AM HOPELESS)	QUESTIONS TO FIND OUT THE THOUGHTS, OPINIONS & WANTS OF OTHERS	ASSUMPTIONS

ASSESS YOUR COMMUNICATION STYLE

Passive:

- ❖ Can't Speak Up
- ❖ Don't Know My Rights
- ❖ Get Stepped on, Meek
- ❖ Too Accommodating, Appeasing
- ❖ Talk Softly, No Eye Contact
- ❖ Gives "Cold Fish" Hand Shakes
- ❖ Don't Stand Up for My Rights, Sulking
- ❖ Avoid Conflicts, Submissive, Flights
- ❖ People Take Advantage of Me

Aggressive:

- Violate Others' Rights Using Power, Position & Language
- Pushy, Dominating
- Must Get My Way
- React Instantly, Fight
- Can Be Abusive, Talking Down
- Out of Control, Emotion
- Don't Care Where or When I 'Blast' Someone

Assertive:

- Direct
- Honest
- Respect Right of Others
- Confident
- Realise I Have Choices
- Effective Communicator
- Can Express My Views
- Make Good Eye Contact
- Speak With Firm Voice

CHARACTERISTICS OF BEHAVIOUR		
PASSIVE	ASSERTIVE	AGGRESSIVE
FAILS TO (OR INDIRECTLY) EXPRESS NEEDS & FEELINGS	DIRECT EXPRESSION OF NEEDS & FEELINGS	DIRECT EXPRESSION OF NEEDS & FEELINGS (TO A FAULT)
AVOID EYE CONTACT	LOOKS DIRECTLY AT OTHERS	USES INTIMIDATING EYE CONTACT
HESITANT OR RAPID SPEECH	FLUID SPEECH PATTERNS	SPEECH MAY BE RAPID RETALIATORY
LOW VOICE	CLEAR, MODULATED VOICE	VOICE MAY BE LOUD OR INTENTIONALLY LOW

CHARACTERISTICS OF BEHAVIOUR		
PASSIVE	**ASSERTIVE**	**AGGRESSIVE**
TENSE BODY MOVEMENTS	CALM BODY POSTURES	TENSE BODY POSTURE; MAY USE THREATENING MOVEMENT
TENDS TO INVITE AGGRESSION FROM OTHERS	NON-THREATENING TO OTHERS	THREATENING TO OTHERS; INVITES COUNTER AGGRESSION
DOES NOT SPEAK UP FOR SELF	STANDS UP FOR LEGITIMATE RIGHTS	IMPINGES ON OTHERS RIGHTS
DEPENDS ON OTHERS TO TAKE CARE OF SELF	ASSUMES RESPONSIBILTY FOR SELF	BLAMES OTHERS (DOES NOT ASSUME RESPONSIBILTY FOR SELF)
	USES 'I' STATEMENTS	

INTROSPECTION QUESTIONNAIRE

1. Do you consider yourself as: Passive, Assertive or Aggressive Person?

   _____

   _____

2. Whether your communication is assertive? How do you know?

   _____

   _____

3. What are the advantages of an aggressive person in business?

   _____

   _____

4. What are areas should a passive business person improve?

   _____

   _____

5. "Am I Assertive?"

   _____

   _____

Chapter – 16

First you learn then you remove the "L"

Learning • Listening • Reading

Reasons for Business Persons to Read

A. LEARNING

For some people college education need not mean a learning process, it can mean failed attempts, changing subjects, failed relationships and everything that you didn't want to do to get a good job. However what a college or a university cannot teach, can be learnt from a professional life experience. If an entrepreneur is stubborn in one's pursuit, then the entrepreneur can learn from mistakes and finally turn into a successful business person. Given below are some useful tips to become a successful entrepreneur:

Start in a Simple Manner: To begin with an illustration, a successful NBA basketball player doesn't straight away start by shooting the ball from the middle of the court, instead he begins by learning the simple nuances of the game. Similarly when starting a business start in a simple manner by trying to learn the basics. Once you identify your niche business interest, slowly start working upwards to design a goal, a plan of action and move forward. Try to identify a unique aspect of your intended business so that you stand out from others.

Select the Right Training Method: Having selected your area of business activity, make sure that you get the right training and mentorship. This will make sure that you get to meet the right kind of people who may be involved in businesses or activities that are similar to what you want to do. Even as you try to gather more information or training about a particular business, you can try shadowing a successful entrepreneur in that business or service so that you can learn valuable lessons that you can implement in your proposed business activity.

Outsourcer: Before getting fully involved in a business activity, you can work as an outsourcer working on a freelance basis. This will give you the time and width to learn more about the business. For example, a manufacturer can initially be an outsourcer for a big ticket label firm before launching his own brand. This will give you a feel of the market and also help you learn all the nuances of the business activity that you want to get into.

Work for the Competitor: There have been instances of an employee of a company quitting his job and launching a similar business venture to become a competitor of his former boss. This might work well in a market where there is a huge demand for a product, sometimes the employer himself may encourage an enterprising employee to become a business person. The employee actually learns the nitty gritties of the business at his former work place and then becomes a successful entrepreneur.

Develop Networks: Successful entrepreneurs have set-up massive networks allowing them to achieve success, which many others have missed. There is no end to what you can accomplish through right networking. Today's technology allows a prospective entrepreneur to build networks offline as well as online through various platforms.

B. LISTENING

Keeping a close ear to your business environment can give you useful tips on becoming a successful entrepreneur or business person.

Busting a Start-Up Myth: A general myth about start-ups is that they are being set-up to make quick money. This is not true, a start-up can only survive if it is launched with a passion for doing something useful in the entrepreneurial world.

Keep an Open Ear for Suggestions: As the owner or head/chief executive officer of a new business organisation you need to keep your ears open for any suggestions. Whether you act upon the suggestion is something different, but the fact you are amenable to listening will make a big difference in the long run.

A Wonderful Idea Is Not the End: Just a spark will not be sufficient to launch a successful business or organisation. Like scientists, business persons will have to work diligently for long hours to convert an idea or a thought into a successful business venture.

Recruit the Right Senior Team: Though some CEOs may think senior staff can be potential threats to their seats, a successful CEO is a person who leads a team of senior staff. So either as an owner or a CEO of a business make sure that you have the right blend of senior staff to take your business or organisation forward.

Do Not Wait to Build Your Business: Sometimes business persons wait for their product or service to become popular before growing their business. On the other hand, some business persons have achieved great success by constantly growing their business by reaching out to potential customers or consumers through advertising platforms.

Emerge as a Good Leader: A vision may be the reason for the birth of a business or organisation, but its growth will depend on good leadership at the top be it a small business or a big organisation.

Be Fast to Adapt to Situations: Markets tend to change with or without reason, a good business organisation is successful if it adapts to the changes as quickly as possible. So keeping a tab on market trends and adapting to situations makes for a good business leader.

Don't Focus Only On Funds: Just thinking that a strong cash balance will lead to the success of your business is a myth. The growth of a business or organisation is measured beyond the availability of cash on hand. In fact, some business even without strong liquidity can be successful by tapping required funds through appropriate sources at the right moment, including through venture capitalists. So focussing only on cash as the measure of success will not be the right mantra for the growth of a business or an organisation.

Why Businesses Fail?: Either the business is too fast too early or the business is too slow to react to changing needs. Being relevant to the market is the most crucial for a business to sustain in a competitive market.

Selling An Established Business: The decision to sell an established business may be taken on the spur of the moment, but one needs to understand that the business or organisation has earned a reputation through years of hard work by the promoters of the business and the staff involved in the organisation.

Actively Keeping Ears Open:

Identify Problems When They Are Nascent: Very often a small matter can snowball into a big issue. So it is essential to identify a problem at the earliest stage and work out remedial measures. Keeping an eye on the processes of your business system and frequently interacting with staff involved in the processes will help you keep a tab on routine issues and nip potential problems in the bud. Sometimes a staff member may be overburdened due to some force of circumstances and if you are in control of the situation, you will immediately assign additional staff to ease the situation instead of allowing the overburdened staff to wilt under pressure.

Be Open to New Ideas: New ideas can flow into your business from any quarter, so it is imperative for you to be amenable to accept the same. If you are rigid then some staff may hesitate to approach you even if they have a good idea to improve your business. Regular interaction with your staff may help you unearth some innovative thoughts or ideas that can really help your business or organisation grow.

Spend Quality Time with Your Staff: Spending quality time with staff will give you an amazing experience of how much information they have about your business and how they have thought of new or innovative ideas to improve the same. Create an atmosphere for your staff to share their thoughts without fear of reprisal or rebuke.

Make Your Clients and Partners Feel Valued: Any strong customer relationship can be built on listening to the views of customers. Especially when customers approach you with a problem make sure that you give a patient hearing instead of dismissing them with rehearsed sales talk. Similarly listening to your business partners and investing time with them can help you grow your business exponentially.

Give Your Employees a Sense of Belonging: Employees are a great asset of a business or an organisation if they are properly utilised. Listening to your staff, especially sales staff who are in constant interaction with consumers, can be of great help to understand in which direction your business is heading. When you start the culture of listening to employees and reacting positively to their ideas, then the employees will start listening to you. However busy your business commitments keep you, earmark time to listen to your staff and if possible interact with some of your customers. The honest opinions from such conversations can help your business to grow immensely.

C. READING

According to a significant Chinese proverb "A cup that is complete is vain," which can mean that there is always scope for adding something. This may be true for the business community. It is always good to remain updated in your business domain. According to 19th century American preacher William Ellery Channing, "It is chiefly through books that we enjoy intercourse with superior minds. In the best books, great men talk to us, give us their most precious thoughts, and pour their souls into ours."

Very often some books may seem irrelevant or unimportant. But updating oneself in the business domain has many advantages. Some global experiences can help business replicate the model to achieve immense success.

Reasons for a Business Person to Read:

- You will not be outdated and can keep abreast of emerging trends in the global scenario. With business situations changing very fast, you may be left behind if you are not aware of current trends.
- As an entrepreneur, you ought to keep your eyes open for opportunities and you might come upon a right business opportunity that you can exploit.
- Reading can also help you assess results of analysis of businesses similar to your venture or organisation. The information gained from such analysis can give you a competitive edge as you can quickly reorient strategies to meet changing market demands.
- Reading can help you to analyse market situations and gain knowledge about markets. While contractors and staff have specialise skills, an entrepreneur is a jack of all trades and by constant reading he can gain immense insights about his business and business practices.

What Type of Books or Articles to Read:

- Read industrial magazines associated with your business activity so that you may be privy to changes in that business segment.
- You can read general business books, magazines or journals to see if you can spot a new area of interest.
- You can read books, magazines and journals that focus on investment issues so that you can implement some of the best practices in your line of activity.
- Read articles, blog posts and books published by your mentors.
- Read autobiographies and biographies of successful business persons to learn from their experiences.
- You can read newspapers to know about what is happening in society keeping in mind societal issues are business opportunities for smart marketers.
- Ultimately and most significantly, read Holy Books to seek God's guidance.

Before concluding, I want to encourage you to improve your analysing ability, because every time I read a book I analyse something new.

Before I end, I want to remind you that **"*Readers are Leaders!*."**

INTROSPECTION QUESTIONNAIRE

1. Whether basic knowledge is necessary to start a new business?
   _____
   _____

2. Why do some corporate companies fail in their business?
   _____
   _____

3. What is 'Active Listening' and specify its advantages.
   _____
   _____

4. Why readers are considered as best leaders?
   _____
   _____

5. How will listening make you a successful entrepreneur?
   _____
   _____

INDEX OF WEBSITES FROM WHICH CONTENT HAS BEEN BORROWED

https://www.entrepreneur.com/article/296664

https://yourstory.com/2016/08/karsanbhai-patel-nirma/

http://www.jyothireddy.com/story.php

https://yourstory.com/2016/08/nitin-godse/

http://t.eaesp.fgvsp.br/en/teaching-knowledge/departments/APOI

https://www.webstrategiesinc.com/blog/selling-strategies-5-proven-networking-techniques

http://www.mhi.org/fundamentals/material-handling

https://www.investopedia.com/terms/d/distribution-channel.asp

http://www.marketing-schools.org/types-of-marketing/traditional-marketing.html

http://customerthink.com/10-ways-to-improve-customer-loyalty/

https://www.investopedia.com/terms/r/returnoninvestment.asp

http://www.smarta.com/advice/sales-and-marketing/sales/develop-a-sales-strategy/

https://www.entrepreneur.com/article/247574

https://www.thebalancesmb.com/choosing-products-to-sell-2890471

https://www.forbes.com/sites/brucekasanoff/2014/07/21/people-are-what-matter-most-in-business/#28516d857647

https://www.inc.com/matt-ehrlichman/the-8-principles-of-customer-delight.html

https://www.leanmethods.com/resources/articles/what-business-system-and-why-do-you-need-one/

https://www.boxtheorygold.com/blog/bid/26268/so-what-exactly-is-a-business-systemhttps://www.boxtheorygold.com/blog/bid/26268/so-what-exactly-is-a-business-system

https://www.infoentrepreneurs.org/en/guides/use-innovation-to-grow-your-business

https://www.allaboutcareers.com/careers/career-path/corporate-training-team-building

https://www.thebalancecareers.com/communication-skills-list-2063779

www.ingramcontent.com/pod-product-compliance
Lightning Source LLC
Chambersburg PA
CBHW031051180526
45163CB00002BA/784